GREAT WALKS

# BRECON BEACONS
## & PEMBROKESHIRE COAST

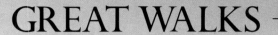

GREAT WALKS

# BRECON BEACONS
# & PEMBROKESHIRE COAST

ROGER THOMAS

Photography by David Ward

Series Editor Frank Duerden

Ward Lock Limited · London

First Published in Great Britain in 1989
by Ward Lock Limited, 8 Clifford Street
London W1X 1RB, a Cassell Company.

Map artwork by Peter Bull Art


Text filmset in Perpetua
by M & R Computerised Typesetting Ltd., Grimsby

Printed and bound in Spain by Graficromo S.A.

**British Library Cataloguing in Publication Data**
Thomas, Roger, 1947–
    Brecon Beacons and Pembrokeshire Coast.—
(Great walks)
    1. South Wales, — Visitors' guide
    I. Title   II. Series
    914.29′404858

    ISBN 0-7063-6716-2

1.  Half-title page: *Porth-clais harbour, near
St David's, Pembrokeshire*

2.  Title-page: *Cribyn and the Beacons' swooping,
north-facing escarpment from Pen y Fan*

# CONTENTS

# ACKNOWLEDGMENTS

In preparing this book, I received assistance and guidance from staff at the Brecon Beacons National Park and the Pembrokeshire Coast National Park. In particular, I would like to thank Roger Stevens, Alan Ward and their colleagues at Brecon, and George Yeomans at Haverfordwest. Elinor Gwynn, The National Trust's warden for the Preseli district of Pembrokeshire, also supplied me with helpful information.

Greatest thanks of all must go to Colin Horsman, a friend and fellow-walker who gave me invaluable help with the Brecon Beacons routes. Colin moved from civilized Sussex to a remote cottage in the shadow of the Black Mountain. Remarkably, he does not seem so far to have suffered any symptoms of culture shock. Much as it goes against the grain to admit it, in the relatively short time he has been living in Wales (five years in comparison to my forty) the knowledge he has acquired of the Beacons puts most of us locals to shame.

I would also like to thank Jill Morgan and Greg Nuttgens for putting me (and my tribe) up at their delightful old farmhouse known as Carnachenwen near Mathry on the north Pembrokeshire coast —and for drying out our clothes so effectively after repeated inundations by the Pembrokeshire rain. They have guest accommodation at their farm, which is close to some of the most fascinating stretches of the Pembrokeshire Coast Path. Jill knows everything about Pembrokeshire past and present, so you will not find a better place to stay—or source of information—when you are walking in this beautiful area.

Thanks also to Jill for accompanying me on a very wet and misty walk to the summit of Carn Ingli. And I cannot finish without a note of gratitude to my family: Liz for meeting me with the car—a welcome sight—at the end of the linear walks, Huw (a dedicated walker) for keeping me company in monsoon conditions on the south Pembrokeshire cliffs, and young Owain—whose idea of a long walk is a stroll around the supermarket shelves—for complaining almost every step of the way on the footpath around the Dale Peninsula.

# INTRODUCTION

There is a hint of vanity in the title of this book. 'Great Walks,' I hear you say. 'How can he justify such a description?' My task in choosing these walks—and making sure that they measure up to the superlative standard implicit in the book's title—was made a little easier, paradoxically, by the fact that I was dealing with *two* National Parks: the Brecon Beacons and Pembroke-shire. Why easier? Limited choice concentrates the mind wonderfully. The selection process was not quite so tortured when dealing with two National Parks, for the classic—or 'great'—walks almost suggested themselves. To whittle down the countless walking possibilities offered by both the Brecon Beacons and Pembrokeshire to a short-list of only twenty-five was indeed a ruthless process, but one that soon highlighted the walks that did not quite measure up.

My definition of 'greatness' was also conditioned by the need to achieve a reasonable distribution of walks across the whole of the Brecon Beacons and along the Pembrokeshire coast. It was also necessary to make sure that there was a good cross-section of grades available, from very easy routes suitable for all the family to long slogs over high, wild terrain that would satisfy the serious outdoor enthusiast.

Furthermore, I have tried to devise as many circular routes as possible. This is very difficult in a place like Pembrokeshire, where the long-distance path around the coast gives few opportunities for walks which start and finish in the same location. There are some areas, such as the Dale Peninsula and Dinas Island (both featured in the book) where a circular walk can be created by taking a short deviation off the coast path. All that I can say is that the inevitable inconvenience of a linear route will be eclipsed by the stunning cliff scenery and superb stretches of untouched coastline which you will enjoy on these Pembrokeshire walks.

I walked the Pembrokeshire coast in the late spring of 1988. Usually, this is a good time to choose, for the wild flowers are out, the sea-birds are everywhere to be seen, and the weather is normally kind. Climatically, 1988 proved to be the exception to the rule. I still have memories of the rain coming at me horizontally as I walked along the exposed, west-facing cliffs of Dinas Island; of sheltering under a bush with cows for company in a downpour at Stack Rocks; and of one, glorious warm, fresh day, an intimation of summer, when the skies were blue and the breeze was gentle as we walked around the beautiful Dale

Peninsula. Hopefully, your experience of Pembrokeshire —where, to be fair, the climate is much more benign than in most parts of Britain—will be in this latter, sunny mould.

And now for something completely different: the Brecon Beacons National Park. I am lucky enough to live in the park, so was able to research most of the walks on a staggered basis throughout the year. This large upland mass—much of it consistently above 1500 ft (450 m)—has an unpredictable climate. There are days in spring and autumn when the sun can shine strongly through clear blue skies; there are days in summer during which you would be forgiven for thinking that winter had arrived six months early; and there are crisp winter days when walking can be a most exhilarating experience. In short, the weather here is a lottery.

The only serious note of caution I would like to sound concerns the high-level, high-grade routes through the more remote stretches of the Beacons. These are best attempted in reasonably good weather. Mist, rain and winds in these exposed, treeless mountains present a real danger, and even well-equipped, experienced walkers have come unstuck in such conditions.

I will finish with an apology to the photographer, David Ward. We were both anxious to walk a few of the Beacons routes together—not too difficult, one would have thought, considering that David has a house in Herefordshire, just across the border from where I live. But a combination of bad weather (for photography, this time) and various pressing deadlines (for words, as well as photographs) when the light was right meant that it was not to be. Sorry David—perhaps next time.

# THE BRECON BEACONS
# NATIONAL PARK

It is standard practice, among some authors, to start a book with a quotation; an apposite, cleverly chosen quotation, normally from the mouth or pen of someone famous, which encapsulates, in a handful of words, the author's intentions. I should like to exploit this dubious device in a perverse way by quoting a celebrated literary figure—Daniel Defoe of *Robinson Crusoe* fame—who came up with something woefully, wonderfully inappropriate.

Defoe travelled to the Brecon Beacons in 1724 and found them 'horrid and frightful, even worse than those mountains abroad'. Who, in their right mind, after reading this description, would want to go walking in such a place? And why on earth did these frightful mountains ever become a National Park?

In all fairness, Defoe was writing before those quasi-spiritual notions of romance, pioneered by William Wordsworth, began to attach themselves to Britain's high, wild places; and he obviously did not like mountains. Even so, he was unduly harsh on the Beacons. The green swooping crests and smooth, open flanks of these grassy uplands are harmonious rather than horrid; they lack, under most climatic conditions, the uncompromising severity that would justify the description 'frightful'.

*The wide, open spaces of the Beacons near Pen y Fan*

The Brecon Beacons, the highest mountains in South Wales, form the nucleus of a National Park that came into existence in 1957, the last of Britain's ten parks. It covers a large area of upland landscape—519 sq miles (134,400 hectares)—all the way from the Welsh border almost to Swansea's doorstep, a distance of over 40 miles (65 km). The boundaries of this National Park are straightforward enough, lacking the apparent arbitrariness exhibited by others and containing in their configuration a clue to the park's creation. The eastern boundary coincides neatly with the Wales–England border, the northern with the Usk Valley and the Mynydd Epynt military range, the western with the verdant Vale of Tywi, and the southern with the beginnings of the industrial and urban conurbations of the Welsh valleys, which pose a threat to the inviolate landscapes so close by.

Geologically, this large slice of South Wales is also quite straightforward. The underlying rock is mainly old red sandstone. The confusion begins only when we come to the terminology, for although the National Park is named after the Brecon Beacons, the Beacons are only one of four mountain ranges within the park boundaries. Matters are further confused by the fact that two of the mountain ranges share almost identical names. So, to put the record straight, the Brecon Beacons National Park consists of the borderland Black Mountains, the central Brecon Beacons, Fforest Fawr, and the western Black Mountain (singular).

The National Park Authority is charged with performing that difficult balancing act between conservation and recreation. It has the usual powers of planning: the Park Committee, made up of twenty-seven members from various county and district councils, together with appointees of the Secretary of State for Wales, assumes, in effect, the responsibility of the local planning authority for the area. The National Park Authority is also concerned with the provision and management of amenities such as visitor centres, car-parks, picnic sites, guided walks, a warden service and so on, as well as with forward planning and research.

As far as the visitor to the area is concerned, by far the best introduction to the National Park is to be found near Libanus, a village a few miles south of Brecon. On Mynydd Illtyd Common above the village stands the Brecon Beacons Mountain Centre. Opened by the National Park in 1966, it serves at least three roles, being an informative starting-point for first-time visitors to the park, giving a comfortable armchair view across to Pen y Fan—at 2906 ft (900 m) the highest peak in South Wales—and providing refreshment for weary walkers.

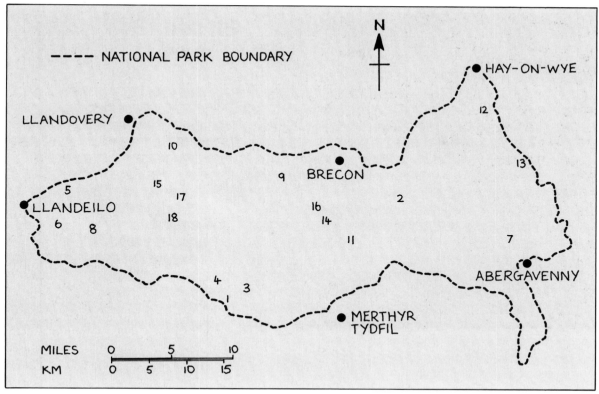

*FIGURE 1  The Brecon Beacons National Park. The numbers indicate the approximate starting points of the walks.*

## SOME FACTS AND FIGURES ABOUT THE BRECON BEACONS NATIONAL PARK

| | |
|---|---|
| DESIGNATED | 1957. It was the last to be designated of the ten National Parks in England and Wales. |
| AREA | 519 sq miles (134,400 hectares). |
| EMBLEM | A flaming beacon burning in a brazier. |
| POPULATION | According to the 1981 census, the total resident population was 32,200. |
| TOURISTS | It is estimated that around seven million visits per year are made to the park. Two-thirds are made by day visitors, the remainder by holidaymakers staying for one or more nights. It can be concluded from this breakdown that, although it is the nearest National Park to London and the South-East, the Brecon Beacons attracts substantially more visitors from the South Wales area than from farther afield. |
| WHERE TOURISTS STAY | There is no concentration of tourist accommodation here (unlike for example, the Tenby and Saundersfoot area of the Pembrokeshire Coast National Park). Towns such as Brecon, |

*The Afon Pyrddin in the Brecon Beacons'
limestone country*

Abergavenny and Llandovery have a reasonable selection of
hotels and guest houses, but most of the 12,000 bed spaces in
the park are scattered thinly all over the area—in small towns
and villages, farmhouses, roadside bed-and-breakfast houses and
country inns.

| LAND OWNERSHIP IN 1988 (%) | | |
|---|---|---|
| National Park Authority | | 13.7 |
| Forestry Commission | | 8.1 |
| Welsh Water Authority | | 6.4 |
| National Trust | | 3.5 |
| Nature Conservancy Council | | 0.6 |
| British Coal | | 0.6 |
| Ministry of Defence | | 0.1 |
| British Waterways Board | | negligible |
| Cadw: Welsh Historic Monuments | | negligible |

NB The remainder of the land is mainly in private ownership.
Land in private ownership and Forestry Commission and
National Trust land contain an element of common land. This is
an important feature of the park. In total, common land
accounts for about 36% of the park's area.

| LAND USE 1981–6 (%) | | |
|---|---|---|
| Agricultural holdings | | 48.6 |
| Common grazings | | 35.4 |
| Woodland (Forestry Commission and other woodland) | | 12.9 |
| Water (reservoirs and lakes) | | 0.6 |
| Other | | 2.5 |

# THE FACE OF THE BRECON BEACONS

## A GEOLOGICAL OVERVIEW

There is a purity and simplicity about the mountains of the Brecon Beacons. This is a park of wide, open spaces, unbroken horizons, grassy, gradual hillsides, clearly defined ridges, high plateaux and expansive moorlands. There is a uniformity to this landscape that is absent in, say, the volcanic jumble, the serrated skylines and the intricate, boulder-strewn slopes of Snowdonia in North Wales.

The Brecon Beacons, in topographical terms, are highland pure and simple. But why such a straightforward personality? The answer lies in the soil. The National Park consists largely of old red sandstone, which covers around two-thirds of the land area. It is a softish, sedimentary rock that has weathered to create the smooth, rounded outlines and great humps of hill and mountain that lumber longitudinally across the landscape.

The Beacons also exhibit an unusual consistency of scale. Generally speaking, there are no great accelerations or reversals in height: over half the park's 519 sq miles (134,400 hectares) are over 1000 ft (300 m) high, much of this upland rising gradually to over 2000 ft (600 m) and peaking at just under 3000 ft (900 m). This gives rise to a problem of which walkers need to be constantly aware. In the Beacons, appearances are deceptive. Somehow—possibly because of their smooth, grassy outlines and gradual gradients—the Brecon Beacons do not look like *real* mountains and lack that stark, emphatic aura that surrounds many highland areas.

But make no mistake: these uplands are not benign and unchallenging. The fact that deaths occur among well-equipped soldiers on winter manoeuvres in the Brecon Beacons speaks for itself. The weather is fickle, mists descend very quickly, and on those treeless, exposed slopes there is little shelter from the wind and rain. There is also the danger posed by the one exception to the general rule of gentle gradients. A 'dip' slope rises gently from the south, then suddenly plunges down a steep, north-facing escarpment (a good example can be seen at Pen y Fan, which is poised above a precipitous drop, and also along the Carmarthen Fans above the remote lakes of Llyn y Fan Fach and Llyn y Fan Fawr in the Black Mountain).

*Piews Du near Bannau Sir Gaer in the remote Black Mountain*

Glaciation has played a major role in moulding this landscape. There are textbook examples of glaciation—enough to fill a schoolchild's notebook twice over—to be seen almost everywhere within the park. The Beacons' wide, rounded U-shaped valleys are a legacy of the grinding, erosive passage of the ice-sheets across a landscape that was originally much more angular. Some classical glacial features are evident around Pen y Fan. Just below the peak is the semicircular hollow of Cwm Llwch. This *cwm,* or cirque, was scooped out by the ice-sheets before being flooded by the glacial lake of Llyn Cwm Llwch when the valley was dammed by material from the retreating glacier.

The shady natural amphitheatre of Craig Cerrig-gleisiad, a few miles north-west of Pen y Fan, was again formed by an accumulation of snow and ice in a hollow at the head of a glacier. Farther west, Llyn y Fan Fach and Llyn y Fan Fawr, like Llyn Cwm Llwch, were created by the waters which collected behind the moraines—mounds of boulders and glacial debris—left by the melting ice. Llangorse Lake, a few miles east of Brecon, also has glacial origins. This 1-mile-long (1.6 km) sheet of water, the largest natural lake in South Wales, was partially created by a moraine of bouldery gravel and clay.

## THE GREAT DIVIDE

No other National Park in Britain has a more self-evident, self-determining border than the boundary that runs along the southern rim of the Brecon Beacons. South of the A465 'Heads of the Valleys' road there is industrial South Wales, a corrugation of narrow, tightly packed valleys which once produced the coal that fuelled Britain's Industrial Revolution and pioneered the new technologies of iron- and steel-making.

North of the A465 a sudden, almost unreal change occurs with the beginning of the National Park. The transition from urban to rural is not a gradual, piecemeal process; the valleys do not gently peter out into open countryside. It all happens abruptly, even savagely. In Brynaman, for example, terraced workers' cottages back onto the wilderness of the Black Mountain. Merthyr Tydfil, once the iron and steel capital of the world, presses up against the unspoilt hills of the Taf Fechan and Taf Fawr Valleys. The old steel town of Ebbw Vale is within minutes of the windy, untouched moors of Mynydd Llangynidr and Mynydd Llangatwg.

This great divide has its roots in the underlying geology. The only major deviation from the predominant old red sandstone occurs along the southern boundary of the National Park, where a narrow band of outcropping carboniferous limestone and millstone grit lies between the old red sandstone to the north and the coal measures to the south. The early industrial pioneers must have thanked their lucky stars. Here, in close proximity, lay the three ingredients essential for the smelting of metal—coal, limestone and iron ore—a catalytic coincidence that triggered off an industrial explosion, the devastating effects of which were contained within the communities of the South Wales valleys.

## HISTORY IN THE HILLS

Prehistoric man left his mark in the Brecon Beacons. The Romans came, saw and (almost) conquered. Medieval barons built strategic strongholds to command the valleys. The ebb and flow of history have washed over the region, leaving a residue of fascinating sites.

Chronologically, Fforest Fawr is a good starting-point from which to dip into the history of human habitation in the park. Plentiful evidence of prehistoric settlement, in the form of stones, tumps and mounds, is scattered across the Brecon Beacons. But without the eye of an archaeologist, most are easily missed. Two of the most conspicuous monuments are to be found in the Llia Valley north of the isolated village of Ystradfellte.

Maen Llia, a huge 11-ft-high (3.4 m) single slab of stone, survives from Bronze Age times. It stands, surrounded by empty moorland and with only the sheep for company, at the head of the valley, a few miles north of another monolith known as Maen Madoc. This slender, 9-ft-high (2.7 m) pillar bridges the gap between Celtic and Roman culture, for inscribed on its side in Latin is the message '(The stone) of Dervacus, son of Justus. He lies here'.

The Brecon Beacons, unlike the mountains farther north, were not a no-go area for the Romans, although it may be fair to say that their hold over the upland areas in the Beacons was tentative rather than total. Their Sarn Helen trackway (a section of which is the subject of Route 1.4 on page 39) forges a characteristically single-minded path across the mountains from Coelbren along the south-western border of the park to the Roman fort at Y Gaer, just west of Brecon. Here, there survive well-preserved stretches of wall and an original gateway from a key stronghold that once housed a garrison of 500 soldiers.

The castle-builders of medieval times were less ambitious

than the Romans, preferring to keep well away from the mountains. Carreg Cennen Castle, near Llandeilo, is a sensational exception. This weather-beaten 'eagle's nest' of a fortress, in the foothills of the Black Mountain, teeters on the brink of a sheer limestone cliff. If you have time to visit only one castle in South Wales, then choose Carreg Cennen (the fortress is the focal point of Route 1.6 on page 50).

Other castle ruins, safely located in the more accommodating, gentler lowlands—at Bronllys and Abergavenny, for example—seem positively tame in comparison. Tretower Court and Castle, in a side valley just off the sheltered Vale of Usk, rightly attracts attention as an unusual two-in-one site. A military keep and a manorial house were built side-by-side, architectural reminders of, respectively, times of war and a later period of relative peace.

## FFOREST FAWR—A ROYAL HUNTING GROUND

Visitors to Fforest Fawr, the upland area sandwiched between the central Beacons and the western Black Mountain, invariably ask: where are the trees? This boggy moorland waste is largely devoid of any tree cover (apart from a few patches of conifer plantation). So why the title Forest—or, to be accurate, Fforest? The 'Great Forest of Brecknock' has never been a forest in the contemporary sense of the word (apart, possibly, from in prehistoric times when the area may have been covered in trees). The title derives from the medieval period, when the term 'forest' was used to describe an area used for hunting.

Fforest Fawr's bare moors and mountains, high and exposed, stand mainly above 1500 ft (450 m). Deer and wild boar were the quarry in this royal hunting ground; today, this bleak, marginal terrain is the domain of hardy breeds of hill sheep.

## WOOD AND WATER

Llangorse Lake, the largest natural stretch of water in the Beacons, is quite outnumbered by its man-made neighbours. At the last count, there were no fewer than nineteen reservoirs in the park or on its boundary. The reasons for this proliferation are simple enough: high rainfall in the mountainous catchment areas and heavy local demand from urban South-East Wales. The reservoirs range in size from the 2-mile-long (3 km) Talybont Reservoir to small ponds, and cover, in total over 1480 acres (600 hectares) of land. Most of these waters are to be found along the southern belt of the Brecon Beacons.

Diehard conservationists are often offended by the flooding of valleys and the creation of man-made sheets of water which in some cases have brought an alien quality to the landscape. However, quite apart from meeting the needs of the heavily populated towns and cities to the south, where most of Wales's industrial and commercial activity is based, the reservoirs here make an important contribution to wildlife resources. Talybont, in particular, now serves as an important habitat for migrating birds and in winter is home to large populations of wildfowl (so much so that the reservoir was made a local nature reserve in 1975). Ironically, this peaceful reservoir is also helping nearby Llangorse Lake, troubled by pollutants and speedboats, to maintain its bird populations, since species can easily commute between the two.

Many of the Beacons' reservoirs are encircled by forestry plantations, another landscape feature introduced by the hand of man. The arguments against the ubiquitous, conformist conifer are familiar enough not to require repeating here. In the Brecon Beacons, commercial forests clothe over 30,000 acres (12,000 hectares), or more than 8% of the total area of the National Park. This acreage represents double the amount of natural broad-leaf and mixed-woodland cover.

The years between the World Wars saw the first serious planting, followed by a further spread in the 1950s and '60s. As is the case with the reservoirs, the impact of the plantations is largely confined to the southern dip slopes, though they have also spread to more isolated areas such as the uplands around the Usk Reservoir in the west and extensive tracts of the Black Mountains in the east.

The march of the conifer does bring some benefits for leisure. The Forestry Commission has, in more recent times, taken a whole series of initiatives to open up its woodlands for recreational purposes. For example, at Garwnant, a few miles north of Merthyr Tydfil, there is an attractive visitors' centre overlooking the Llwyn-on Reservoir with waymarked walks, a children's adventure playground and picnic sites. Other forests, particularly in the Ponsticill area, have similar facilities which, although probably a curse to the serious hill-walker, do provide a gentle introduction to the countryside which many city-dwelling families appreciate.

## COMMON LAND

One of the great glories of the Brecon Beacons is its extensive

*Sugar Loaf summit above Abergavenny*

areas of open hill and mountain land across which walkers can roam. The sense of openness and freedom enjoyed by walkers is largely attributable to the high proportion of common land—over a third of the total land area—within the park. But there are many misconceptions about common land. The public do not have, as a matter of course, right of access to common land (except on public rights-of-way) unless this is specifically granted under some enactment. In lowland areas and along the urban fringes, commons are often areas where the chief use today is public recreation. In the uplands (where all the serious walking takes place), grazing remains their main function.

But the good news is that the public has rarely been prevented from walking at will over this common land in the National Park. This is because of a valuable tradition, known as *de facto* access, which has become established in the area. Should it ever be challenged, it would be defended by the National Park Authority. The National Trust's role is also important here. It is obliged by law to allow the public onto its commons, including terrain much patronized by walkers in the central Beacons range and the Sugar Loaf, above Abergavenny.

# Selected Walks in the Brecon Beacons National Park

*Spectacularly located Carreg Cennen Castle teeters on the edge of a limestone cliff in the foothills of the Black Mountain*

# INTRODUCTION TO THE ROUTE DESCRIPTIONS

1. ACCESS (see pages 170 and 173)

In the Brecon Beacons the major part of the extensive common land is accessible to the public either through legal right of access or *de facto* access (see page 18).

Along the Pembrokeshire coast, matters are much more straightforward. Nearly all the walks featured in this book follow sections of the long-distance Pembrokeshire Coast Path, opened in 1970, along which there is a public right-of-way for its entire length.

Short-cuts which might lead to a proliferation of paths or to the annoyance of local people should not be taken. But you may find (especially in the Beacons) that a path has been diverted officially by the National Park Authority, perhaps to allow a badly eroded section to recover. The diversion will usually be well marked and should always be followed.

2. ASCENT

The amount of climbing involved in each route in the Beacons has been estimated from Outdoor Leisure 1:25 000 maps and should be regarded as approximate only. Except in the case of one Pembrokeshire walk—to Carn Ingli in the Preseli Hills, the ascent of which has been estimated from a Pathfinder 1:25 000 map—the nature of the coastal terrain makes ascent information irrelevant.

3. CAR-PARKS

In most cases, walks start from a convenient car-park. If there is no official place to park, then there will be good space to leave your vehicle. If you are parking by the wayside please choose a space carefully, so as not to inconvenience local people.

4. INTERESTING FEATURES ON THE ROUTE

The best position for seeing these is indicated both in the route descriptions and on the maps by *(1)*, *(2)*, etc.

5. LENGTH

These are strictly 'map miles' estimated from the Outdoor Leisure and Pathfinder (1:25 000) and Landranger (1:50 000) series. No attempt has been made to take into account any ascent or descent involved.

6. MAPS

The maps are drawn to a scale of 1:25 000 and names are as given on the appropriate Outdoor Leisure, Pathfinder or Landranger maps. Field boundaries in particular, which can be a

*FIGURE 2 Symbols used on the route maps.*

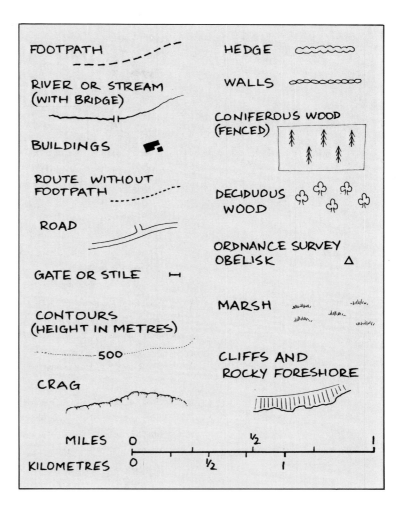

mixture of hedge, fence and wall, should be taken as a 'best description'. The maps have been drawn, wherever possible, so that the reader goes from the bottom to the top of the page. This will enable the reader to 'line up' the map in the direction walked while still holding the book in the normal reading position. The arrow on each map points to grid north. The scale of some small features has been slightly exaggerated for clarity. For easy cross-reference, the relevant Outdoor Leisure or Pathfinder sheets are indicated on each map.

7. ROUTE DESCRIPTION

The letters 'L' and 'R' stand for left and right respectively. Where they are used for changes of direction then they imply a turn of about 90° when facing in the direction of the walk. 'Half L' and 'half R' indicate a half-turn, i.e. approximately 45°, and 'back half L' or 'back half R' indicate three quarter-turns, i.e. about 135°. PFS stands for 'Public Footpath Sign' (which usually appears as 'Llwybr Cyhoeddus' in Wales) and OS for 'Ordnance

Survey'.

To avoid constant repetition, it should be assumed that all stiles and gates mentioned in the route descriptions are to be crossed (unless there is a specific statement to the contrary).

## 8. STANDARD OF ROUTES

The briefest examination of the route descriptions that follow will show that the routes cover an enormous range of both length and difficulty. The easiest can probably be undertaken by a family party at almost any time of the year, while the hardest are only suitable for experienced hill-walkers who are both fit and well-equipped. Any walker who is contemplating following a route should make sure before starting that it is within his or her capability.

It is not easy in practice, however, to give an accurate picture of the difficulty of any route because it is dependent upon a number of factors and will in any case vary considerably from day to day with the weather. Any consideration of weather conditions must, of course, be left to the walker himself (but read the section on safety on page 171 before setting off). Apart from that, it is probably best to attempt an overall assessment of difficulty based upon the length, amount of ascent and descent, problems of route-finding and finally, upon the roughness, remoteness and exposed nature of the terrain.

Each of the routes has therefore been given a grading based upon a consideration of these factors. A grade appears as the first of the numerals above the title of each walk (the second numeral relates to the walk's number, the walks being numbered consecutively throughout the book). A general description of each grade follows (please note that the mileages for each grade are only rough guidelines; some walks of limited length may have been given a higher grade because of, for example, the severity of the route).

*Easy* (1): Generally short walks (up to 5 miles/8 km) over well-defined paths, suitable for a family party (although children must be kept in close control by adults on certain sections of cliff-top path on the Pembrokeshire Coast Path). Route-finding should present no problem. The ascent of some slopes may be involved, but this will be mostly over fairly gradual inclines, with only short sections of more difficult ground.

*Moderate* (2): Rather longer walks (up to about 9 miles/14 km) mostly over paths but with sections where route-finding will be more difficult. Upland areas may involve steeper and rougher ground. These walks are suitable for most ordinary ramblers.

*More strenuous* (3): These are in many cases longer walks, although their main feature is their more arduous nature. There may be prolonged spells of climbing and some rough ground,

*St Non's Well near St David's, Pembrokeshire*

calling for good route-finding ability, perhaps with stretches of scrambling. These routes are designed for stronger walkers who are fit and walk fairly regularly.

*Very strenuous* (4): There is one Grade 4 walk in this book, a long route across the remote, difficult terrain of the Black Mountain in the western Brecon Beacons. This should only be attempted by experienced outdoor enthusiasts, such as active members of the Long Distance Walkers Association and should be regarded as a real challenge.

The walks are arranged in order of increasing difficulty for both National Parks, beginning with 1 (the easiest) in each case.

A summary of each walk appears above each detailed description, giving information on length, amount of climbing involved (where appropriate) and any special difficulties such as dangerous cliffs or scrambling, that will be met along the way.

## 9. STARTING AND FINISHING POINTS

The majority of the routes are circular in order to avoid any problem with transport when the walk is completed. Unfortunately, in the case of a few of the ridge walks in the Brecon Beacons and most of the walks along the Pembrokeshire coast, it is impossible to devise circular routes. The location of each starting (and finishing) point is given by the number of the appropriate Outdoor Leisure or Pathfinder map (1:25 000 scale) with a six-figure grid reference see 'Giving a Grid Reference' on page 172).

## 10. TIME FOR COMPLETION

The usual method of estimating the length of time needed for a walk is Naismith's Rule: 'For ordinary walking allow one hour for every 3 miles (5 km) and add one hour for every 2000 feet (600 m) of ascent; for backpacking with a heavy load allow one hour for every 2½ miles (4 km) and one hour for every 1500 feet (450 m) of ascent.' However, for many this tends to be over-optimistic and it is better for each walker to form an assessment of his or her own performance over one or two walks. Naismith's Rule also makes no allowance for rest or food stops or for the influence of weather conditions.

# 1.1

# SGWD GWLADUS
# WATERFALL WALK

**STARTING AND FINISHING
POINT**
Parking area near Angel Inn at the
village of Pontneddfechan
(Outdoor Leisure Sheet 11/901076)
**LENGTH**
2½ miles (4 km)

This delightful walk, along the beautiful wooded valley to the waterfall of Sgwd Gwladus, is suitable for all the family (though little children should be kept under control at all times, as the path runs beside a fast-flowing river). It serves as a perfect introduction to the limestone scenery—with its attendant wooded gorges, tumbling rivers and falls—that can be found along the southern rim of the National Park. The walk is full of interest, both in terms of its industrial archaeology and its natural beauty. Take something to eat with you and take advantage of the plentiful picnic sites along the way.

## ROUTE DESCRIPTION (Map 1)

There are many places to park the car in the general area around the Angel Inn. The entrance to the walk is just behind the inn, beside the old stone bridge over the River Neath (Afon Nedd). Go past the barrier marked 'Sgwd Gwladus Lady Waterfalls' and follow the path along the western bank. The pathway here, elevated high above the river, soon skirts a massive, overhanging rocky outcrop known as the Farewell Rock (1). The path (2), well engineered and wide, is much better than the usual riverside walk—a legacy, no doubt, of the fact that it follows an old tramway for about the first ⅔ mile (1 km).

Within ¼ mile (400 m) or so of the start, you will come to the ruins of a corn mill (3), after which the riverside opens out a little into a grassy field. The valley sides soon close in again to reveal evidence of old mine workings (4). Just north of the mines, where the stream running down from Cwm Gored joins the Neath, there is a most attractive picnic site set in a leafy riverside glade.

From here, the path becomes much narrower as it climbs a short series of steps up into the steep hillside above the river. Within about ¼ mile (400 m) of the picnic site you will come to a large pool at the confluence of the Neath and Pyrddin rivers.

*The ruined mill beside the Afon Nedd*

24

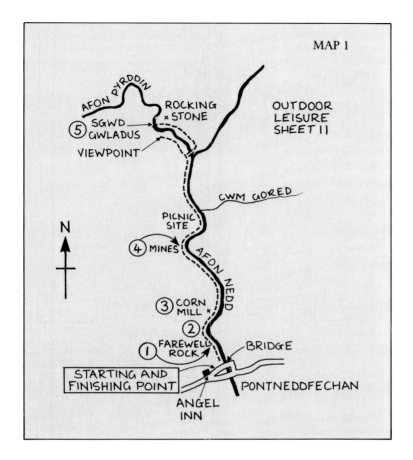

MAP 1

AFON PYRDDIN

ROCKING × STONE

OUTDOOR LEISURE SHEET II

⑤ SGWD GWLADUS

VIEWPOINT

CWM GORED

PICNIC SITE

④ MINES

AFON NEDD

③ CORN MILL ×

②

① FAREWELL ROCK

BRIDGE

STARTING AND FINISHING POINT

ANGEL INN

PONTNEDDFECHAN

N

You have two choices here. Stay on the L bank of the river (do not go over the footbridge) signposted 'Sgwd Gwladus Viewing Platform' and follow the Pyrddin as it flows down a rocky staircase of small falls to the picnic site and view-point which looks across to the major fall of Sgwd Gwladus *(5)*.

If you prefer, you can get even nearer to the waterfall by crossing the footbridge and turning half L along the opposite bank of the Pyrddin. This muddy path initially climbs the hillside, then drops down to a pretty clearing beside the riverbank just below the fall. You can climb up past the little log cabin and picnic site to the top of the fall, but do not go near the edge of the overhanging ledge.

From here, retrace your steps back to Pontneddfechan.

*1 Farewell Rock*

This dark, concave rock face is so called after the colloquial name for hard, close-grained sandstone. This sandstone forms the upper levels of the millstone grits found along the southern rim of the National Park. Its local name is most expressive; in geological sequence, the rock lies below the coal measures, so when miners struck this sandstone with their pick axes, they knew they had bid farewell to their coal seams.

2 *The pathway*

The route beside the River Neath in this first section of the walk follows the course of an old tramway. Horse-drawn trams would haul silica from the mines, sunk into the sides of the valley, to Pont Walby over ¾ mile (1.2 km) south-east of Pontneddfechan. From here, cargoes were carried 14 miles (22 km) by barge along the Neath Canal to Briton Ferry and the sea.

3 *The Old Mill*

These are the overgrown and quite extensive ruins of a double-race mill that was used by local farmers to grind corn.

4 *Silica mines*

Both banks of the river were mined for silica. Mining activity here was extensive—and quite prosperous—from the early 1820s up until the turn of the century. The valley sides bear plentiful evidence of mining, an enterprise based on the fact that fire-bricks of exceptional quality and value could be made from this local 'Dinas Silica'. Silica bricks were made at Pont Walby until 1920. In its heyday, Dinas fire-brick was known all over Europe and America, its exceptional properties making it ideal for lining iron- and steel-making furnaces and lime kilns as well as domestic fireplaces.

5 *Sgwd Gwladus*

This waterfall is on the Pyrddin, a tributary of the River Neath. It has an almost primeval quality to it, a product of its gloomy, mossy and atmospheric setting beneath tall, dark cliffs. At the top of the fall there is a flat platform of rock, which overhangs the pool below a little. Keep away from this dangerous ledge—there is a fine view of the fall from the poolside. When the river is low, you may be able to scramble to a point behind the waterfall, but this is never as accessible as the path that runs behind the famous fall of Sgwd yr Eira on the Afon Hepste (see Route 1.3, page 33).

Sgwd Gwladus is reputedly named after Gwladus, one of the twenty-five daughters of Brychan, a fifth-century chieftain who ruled Brycheiniog (which became, in time, Brecknock or Breconshire). The waterfall is also known as the Lady's Fall. On the eastern side of the fall there is a huge boulder. This was a carefully balanced rocking stone (it is claimed you could crack nuts beneath it) until a gang of workmen dislodged it in the nineteenth century.

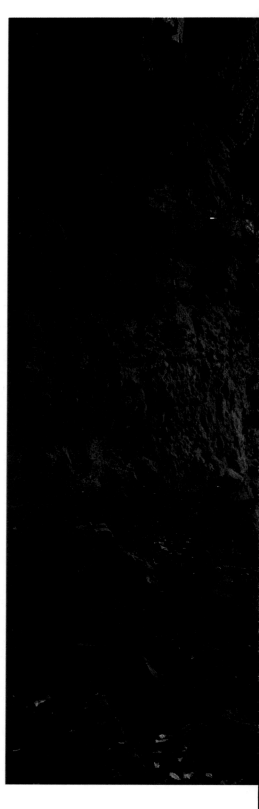

*Sgwd Gwladus, set in a shady, wooded natural amphitheatre*

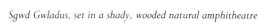

# 1.2

# ALLT YR ESGAIR

**STARTING AND FINISHING POINT**
Picnic site car-park at Talybryn on the A40, ½ mile (0.8 km) south of Llansantffraed (Outdoor Leisure Sheet 11/130227)
**LENGTH**
3½ miles (5.5 km)
**ASCENT**
700 ft (220 m)

A stroll through attractive broad-leaf woodland and superb views across the wide Usk Valley to the Brecon Beacons are the main features of this pleasant walk around the slopes of Allt yr Esgair. The path ascends the hillside in easy stages, to reach an ancient earthwork crowning the open, grass-covered summit. The walk is waymarked for part of the route and suitable for all age groups.

## ROUTE DESCRIPTION (Map 2)

Go through the wooden gate from the car-park into a narrow lane between hedgerows. Turn immediately L through a further gate, then cross over two fields by the marked public path to reach a trackway in a triangle of rough open land, dotted with gorse and bushes. The track divides here. Take the R fork leading into the trees, walking along a narrow, winding path through substantial mixed woodland. To the R of the path, among old quarry workings, are a number of dead trees in various stages of decay. These rotting hulks are elms, the victims of the fatal Dutch elm disease. Walk on past this sad graveyard, cross over a stile, and follow the path through an attractive grove of birch and oak trees *(1)* to a junction by a low stone wall. Turn L along the waymarked track. To your R beyond the fence is a recent tree-planting scheme *(2)*. The National Park has planted this hillside with a variety of trees including oak, hazel and flowering cherry.

Go on through two gates, turning R at a blue waymarker just beyond the second gate. Take the higher parallel track through a small group of mature Scots pine *(3)*, then on along the bottom edge of the woodland for ½ mile (800 m) to a junction. Follow the blue waymarker pointing straight on to reach further direction arrows at a metal gate. Keep R along the main path to find the ruins of the Paragon Tower, a hunting lodge built in 1817 and known locally as Squire Jones's Folly.

The woodland ends just here and a stile beyond the tower leads onto overgrown common land. Go on by the narrow path

*The early nineteenth-century Paragon Tower*

28

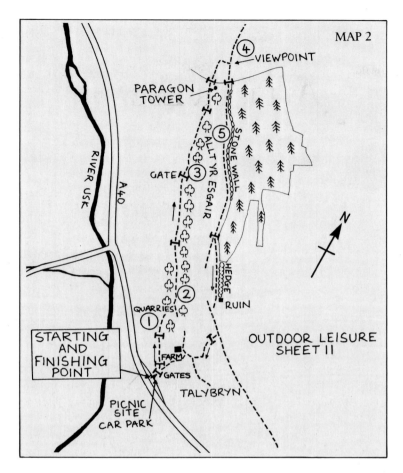

through bushes and small trees to where the scrubland stops at an open expanse of sweeping pasture. Turn sharp R and climb straight uphill toward a line of low bushes above, then on across a rough track to reach a drystone wall. The view beyond comes as quite a surprise. The whole of Llyn Syfaddan (Llangorse Lake) *(4)* is laid out below in a picture-book landscape of tiny fields and woodland.

Go up the sunken path toward the line of conifers and a gate. Do not cross over the stile to the L, but carry on, following the magnificent drystone wall along the forest boundary, then bear slightly R to reach the high view-point on top of Allt Hill. The bright green fields of the wide Usk Valley *(5)* are revealed, stretching both east and west, with the backdrop of the Brecon Beacons behind.

By looking south-east along the top of the hill you will gain a fine perspective of open common land. Set off in this direction, pass through a gate in the stone wall, and go on to the corner of the conifer plantation. Turn L and follow the old track down through the fields along a line of large thorn bushes, past a

Overleaf: *The view into the sheltered Usk Valley from Allt yr Esgair*

ruined building, to join a narrow straight lane between the hedgerows. Turn R at the first junction, go through the wooden gate, then on downhill to reach the attractive working farm of Tal-y-bryn-uchaf. This old lane is a well-preserved example of an original agricultural road, established between farm dwellings in the early nineteenth century.

Just before the farmyard gate turn sharp L, then sharp R to a junction with farm buildings visible on both sides. Continue straight down, passing between two old stone walls into the sunken lane ahead, then on to reach the car-park and your starting-point below.

1 *Birch and oak trees*
The majority of woodland on the Allt hill has been planted over the years for some purpose. This birch grove serves as useful cover for the much slower-growing oaks beneath and will eventually die back, overshadowed by the maturing oak trees. Alternatively the birch, commonly known as the weed tree, may be felled earlier, giving the sturdy young oaks full rein in their domination of the woodland.

2 *Tree-planting schemes*
The National Park provides labour and materials for tree-planting schemes in existing old woodland. Allt Hill is a prime site for the replacement of ageing tree populations and the filling-in of gaps in the woodland canopy.

Tree planting is essential to the well-being of many woodlands because the traditional grazing of sheep among the trees gives the natural seedlings no chance to survive. Consequently, the newly planted trees are fenced off to keep nibbling teeth well away from tasty young saplings.

3 *Scots pines*
This small stand of mature pines was planted about thirty years ago by the landowner, with the intention of eventually felling the trees to provide useful timber. However, the pines still survive, probably because of the prohibitive cost of extraction and the more attractive price of commercially available softwoods.

The landscape of Wales is dotted with these small groves of conifers, often planted close to a farmhouse, on its northern side, thus providing protection from harsh winter storms.

4 *Llyn Syfaddan (Llangorse Lake)*
This ancient glacial lake is a National Nature Reserve and contains several rare species of aquatic plant. However, recreational pressures such as those caused by power-boating and water-skiing, together with pollution, possibly derived

from agricultural fertilizers, are a serious disturbance to the delicate ecology of the lake, threatening both bird and plant life. The only hope must lie in greater control and management of this beautiful lake.

The tiny island at the western end is man-made, constructed from tree trunks and stones during the Bronze Age, probably as a refuge from wild animals.

5 *Usk Valley*

Running almost the whole length of the National Park, the Usk Valley is a major geographical feature and contains some of the area's best farmland. The Brecon Beacons follow the course of the valley westward and the summits of Pen y Fan and Corn Du can be seen to the right. Straight ahead is the village of Talybont-on-Usk, with the deep-cut valley of the Talybont Forest and Reservoir behind. The tall conical hill to the left of Talybont is bare-topped Tor y Foel, the last outpost of the Beacon range.

*Woodland along the flanks of Allt yr Esgair*

# THE WATERFALLS WALK

STARTING POINT
Small parking area on western fringes
of the village of Penderyn (Outdoor
Leisure Sheet 11/944089)
FINISHING POINT
Porth yr Ogof car-park (Outdoor
Leisure Sheet 11/928124)
LENGTH
3¼ miles (6 km)

'Waterfall Country', as it is known, is a distinctive corner of the Brecon Beacons National Park. Its shady, thickly wooded limestone gorges, waterfalls and cave systems are a claustrophobic antidote to those wide, open, agoraphobia-producing spaces which characterize the park. This walk, which follows the Hepste and Mellte rivers, takes in four magnificent waterfalls (the highlight of the route is the path that leads behind one of them). Although quite short, it can be extremely muddy and, in sections, rough underfoot, so is not really suitable for very young children.

## ROUTE DESCRIPTION (Map 3)

Follow the PFS along the path past the white-painted cottages and display board which contains a map of the route. Within 300 yards (275 m), where the gravel road turns L, go straight on over a stile. The path then skirts the rocky outcrops of an old quarry. Go straight on, following the waymark at the next junction, where a grassy path drops away half R off the main track. The path then leads into an open area of rough, rocky ground. Follow the waymarking arrows as the path runs, more or less straight on, through the stony ground of these abandoned quarry workings.

Beyond the quarry, the terrain suddenly changes completely, becoming boggy, open moorland. The footpath here can resemble a black, oozing quagmire, so pick your way carefully—and make sure that your boots are well water-proofed. About 300 yards (275 m) after the quarry, cross a small stream and a stile, following the line of the fence uphill in the direction of a gate, beyond which there is a sparse forestry plantation. Bear half R at the gate, keeping the fence to your L as you walk across elevated, open countryside with panoramic views north-eastwards to Pen y Fan, to the empty expanses of Fforest Fawr to the north and, to the west, the open-cast coal workings around Onllwyn on the edge of the National Park.

Cross the stile by the notice-board warning walkers of the

dangerous gorges near the waterfalls and go straight on over another boggy section of moorland between the thinly planted conifers. The path drops gradually downhill towards the thickly wooded, steep-sided gorge in which the Hepste flows, with more spectacular views westwards to the sheer limestone cliffs above the confluence of the Mellte and Hepste.

A scattering of huge boulders, beyond which there is yet another warning sign, marks the point where the path bears R and descends abruptly into the gloomy, craggy gorge by a very steep series of zig-zagging steps cut into the slope. At the bottom is Sgwd yr Eira *(1)* and the most memorable few yards of the walk (especially after heavy rain). This is the section where the path takes advantage of the overhang beneath the waterfall and allows you to walk behind the curtain of water without getting wet (perhaps not strictly true, for the spray can soak you if you linger long enough).

On emerging from beneath the waterfall, follow the indeterminate path downstream for 100 yards (90 m) or so until you come to the series of steps which takes you up and out of the gorge. Turn L at the T-junction at the top of the steep climb and within 15 yards (14 m) turn half R, following the main path up the hill until you come to a conifer-plantation boundary fence. Turn L here, following the path across high ground as it skirts the edge of the forest, passing a fine view-point which looks back down the gorge to Sgwd yr Eira.

The path bears around to the R, still following the line of the forest fence, until you come to a signpost which points downwards to the waterfalls of Sgwd y Pannwr and Sgwd Isaf Clun-gwyn on the Mellte *(2)*. If you wish to see Sgwd y Pannwr at close quarters, then take the path which drops down half L from the main route at this signpost. You will, though, have to retrace your steps back up to the main path after Sgwd y Pannwr, for there is no advised path along the precipitous gorge to Sgwd Isaf Clun-gwyn. (The Brecon Beacons National Park Authority is rightly concerned that walkers should avoid the narrow pathways cut into the near-vertical gorge at this point.)

Having returned to the main 'top' route, follow the line of the forest fence. There are more lofty views along this section, particularly looking back southwards to the Rhigos Mountain, a formidable upland barrier that stands between the National Park and the famous coal-bearing Rhondda Valleys. Above Sgwd Isaf Clun-gwyn, the path bears around to the R, still following the fence (from here there is a spectacular view down into the gorge as far as the third fall, Sgwd Clun-gwyn).

Continue along the well-defined path. Within 400 yards (375 m) of the view-point, yellow route-markers define the path

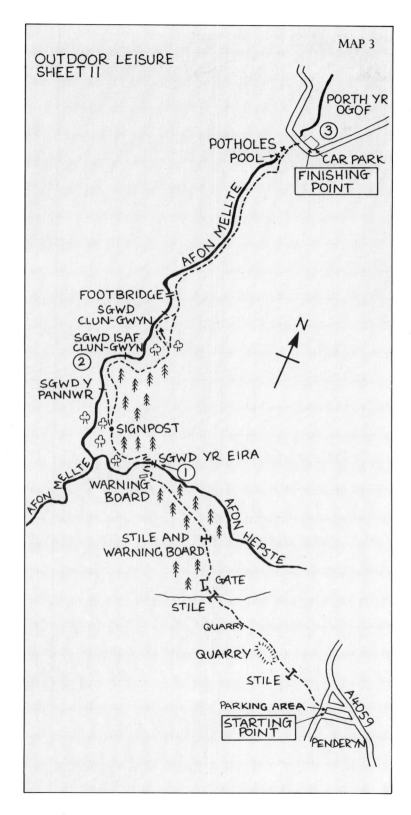

OUTDOOR LEISURE
SHEET 11

MAP 3

PORTH YR
OGOF

POTHOLES
POOL

③

CAR PARK

FINISHING
POINT

AFON MELLTE

FOOTBRIDGE
SGWD
CLUN-GWYN

SGWD ISAF
CLUN-GWYN

②

N

SGWD Y
PANNWR

SIGNPOST

SGWD YR EIRA

①

AFON MELLTE

WARNING
BOARD

AFON HEPSTE

STILE AND
WARNING BOARD

GATE

STILE

QUARRY

QUARRY

STILE

PARKING AREA

STARTING
POINT

A4059

PENDERYN

*Sgwd Clun-gwyn on the Mellte*

along the undulating, wooded hillside. At a junction of two paths, bear L downhill, following the yellow waymarks. The path reaches the river just south of Sgwd Clun-gwyn, then runs along the gorge before climbing up beside the waterfall to the high ground above. Make for the edge of the forest.

Within 150 yards (140 m), turn half L and begin to descend again to the river, crossing a rocky section of path. Follow the riverbank past the footbridge across the Mellte, then walk across a grassy field to pick up the riverbank once again. The path then narrows as it crosses rough, boggy ground before skirting the edge of a field and ultimately opening out into a wide, grassy area on the approach to Porth yr Ogof *(3)*.

Leave the riverbank and pick your way across the polished, irregularly shaped limestone rocks above the dark pool where the Mellte emerges from the cave. The path then runs on the ground above the course of the underground river, which can be heard as it flows past two large pot-holes just off the route. At the surfaced road, turn R and immediately L to the Porth yr Ogof car-park. To view the cave, follow the path down into the gorge from the car-park.

1 *Sgwd yr Eira*

Although not the tallest of the waterfalls in this area, Sgwd yr Eira is undoubtedly the most famous. This is probably because the path hugs the ledge directly beneath the overhang, allowing walkers to venture behind the drop of water. In times gone by, this route was much appreciated by local farmers, who used the ledge to drive their flocks across the river. The novelty of seeing a waterfall from the inside out is possible because a 5-ft (1.5 m) band of soft shales, lying beneath a tougher, thicker band of rock above, has been washed away to create a concavity behind the fall. A wide sheet of water drops 50–60 ft (15–18 m) over Sgwd yr Eira ('The spout of snow') on the Hepste.

Another notable feature of this river valley and the neighbouring Mellte is the outstanding natural woodlands which flourish in these limestone gorges. The woods are mostly of oak, with some birch, alder, ash, hazel and rowan.

2 *Sgwd y Pannwr, Sgwd Isaf Clun-gwyn and Sgwd Clun-gwyn*

These three falls are on the Mellte. They appear within less than a mile (1.6 km) of each other, creating a watery staircase in a steep-sided, thickly wooded gorge. The first of the falls on this walk is Sgwd y Pannwr ('The Fall of the Fuller'). Upstream are the two main falls of the river, Sgwd Isaf Clun-

*A path runs behind Sgwd yr Eira, the famous waterfall on the Hepste*

gwyn ('Lower White Meadow Fall')—the curved top of which is said to resemble a 'miniature Niagara'—and Sgwd Clun-gwyn ('White Meadow Fall').

Geologically, these falls signal a change in the underlying rock structure. Sgwd Clun-gwyn stands on the line where millstone grits (to the south) begin to overlay the limestones (to the north). The grits consist of variable bands of rock and shale which offer varying levels of resistance to erosion. Water flows over the harder, upper beds but erodes the softer shales below to produce rapids and, also under the influence of faulting, waterfalls. The best example of this differential erosion can be seen at Sgwd Isaf Clun-gwyn, where a fault has brought hard and soft millstone grits together.

When these falls are in full spate they make a marvellous sight. In the words of one writer, 'To see them in perfection the traveller must wait for rain . . . For this he need not wait long as the country is seldom two days without showers.'

3 *Porth yr Ogof ('Gateway of the cave')*

This awesome cave entrance, probably the largest in Wales, swallows up the Mellte, the river reappearing ¼ mile (400 m) downstream in a deep, dangerous pool. Watercourses come and go with surprising irregularity along this part of the Mellte, often flowing underground, a phenomenon explained by the underlying rock, carboniferous limestone. This easily soluble rock erodes to produce fissures, pot-holes and caverns, the largest of which is Porth yr Ogof.

Today, the cave is a popular venue for parties of pot-holers. When the river is low, you can venture a very short distance into the cave by walking along a natural platform. In the gloom, you should be able to pick out a white formation. This is a band of white calcite in an otherwise black rock wall. Its shape, which resembles a horse, gives the cavern its alternative name of 'White Horse Cave'. Avoid the temptation to explore this dangerous cave system unless you are properly equipped and in the company of experienced cavers.

*The Mellte flows through a thickly wooded gorge*

# 1.4

# SARN HELEN ROMAN ROAD

STARTING POINT
By the entrance to the forest at the
end of the metalled road running east
from Coelbren (Landranger Sheet
160/879117; this point is just off edge
of Outdoor Leisure Sheet 11, square
8811)
FINISHING POINT
Where Sarn Helen meets metalled
road north of Ystradfellte (Outdoor
Leisure Sheet 11/925166)
LENGTH
4¾ miles (7.5 km) with an optional ¾
mile (1.2 km) diversion
ASCENT
450 ft (140 m)

This is a wonderfully airy walk across the ancient Sarn Helen trackway. Well-defined throughout the route and level for most of the way, the path is suitable for families with children who are enthusiastic walkers (though it is perhaps a little long for the very young). As a counterpoint to the empty, extensive moorlands and huge panoramas along most of the route, there is an optional diversion into the shady river valley carved by the Nedd, leading to the gloomy, chilly pot-hole of Pwll-y-Rhyd.

## ROUTE DESCRIPTION (Maps 4, 5)

Park the car near the entrance to the Coed y Rhaiadr Forest. Go through the gate and follow Sarn Helen (1) across the moorland, with the mature conifer forest to your R and the wide, open, silent moor on your L. For the next mile (1.6 km) or so, the road dips and rises over gently undulating terrain. There are wonderful views eastwards to the central Beacons and the flat-topped peak of Pen y Fan, before the path begins to drop down, where it passes a fire tower, off the high moorland into the forest, with trees on both sides.

The road heads northwards and there is now forest on your L and open countryside to your R. From here, it is interesting to note the contrast between the rounded, treeless slopes of the old red sandstones to the north (archetypal Beacons scenery) and the craggy, wooded, deeply incised valleys of the National Park's limestone country to the south.

At the junction, about 50 yards (45 m) before the gate across Sarn Helen, you can take a detour down into the valley to Pwll-y-Rhyd (2). Turn R off the Roman road, past the deep sink holes that look like bomb craters, and follow the path down through a mossy, wooded glade to the bridge across the river. Cross the bridge and stiles and follow the path down the eastern riverbank, i.e., turn to the R. This is popular pot-holing country—the hillside here is riddled with cave systems.

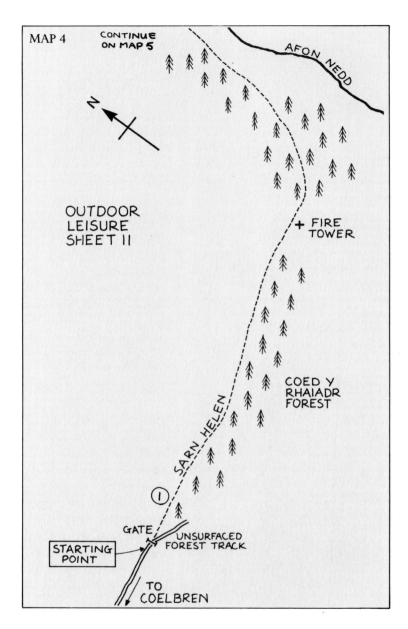

Unless there has been rain, you should be able to walk along the stony riverbed, for in low volumes the Nedd will have by now disappeared underground. After the rains, the river pours into a deep chasm at Pwll-y-Rhyd. This spectacular formation is located 150 yards (140 m) south of the bridge, where the rocky riverbed suddenly funnels into a very narrow gorge, ending up in a shady, cool, water-filled basin lined with huge slabs of limestone broken by vertical fissures. From here, retrace your steps back up to Sarn Helen.

Go through the gate, following Sarn Helen northwards, with

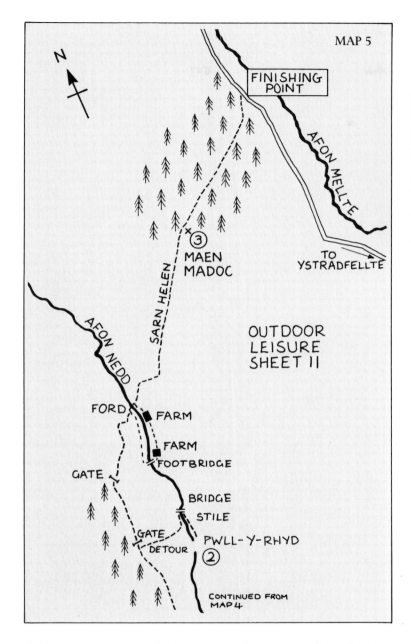

*Looking across the upper reaches of the Nedd Valley*

the forest on your L and a drystone wall on your R. Just after the gate, note the huge sink hole—the biggest of the lot—on your L. At the northern end of the forest, turn R and go through the gate set into the drystone wall, following the Roman road down to the river.

Here, those intent on walking Sarn Helen every step of the way will take off their boots and wade across the ford (not at all unpleasant on a warm day). The owners of the two farms on the opposite bank have come to the rescue of those who do not

Overleaf: *The lonely Maen Madoc standing stone*

wish to get wet feet. They have kindly given permission for walkers to cross their land to gain access to a footbridge across the river 400 yards (375 km) south of the ford.

There are, in fact, a number of permutations of route down from Sarn Helen to this bridge, but the one given below is probably the easiest to follow.

Turn R at the riverside, walking downstream and keeping as close as possible to the river. There is no path here, the ground is quite rough, and you have to cross a partially fallen fence. Stick to this advised route and respect the farmers' property at all times. Opposite the second farm, go across the footbridge which leads into the farmyard. Turn L and follow the road north which connects the two farms and return to the ford and Sarn Helen. Follow the road as it climbs up the open hillside, and within ¼ mile (1.2 km) you will come to Maen Madoc (3). From here, Sarn Helen descends through the trees for another ¼ mile (1.2 km) before meeting the metalled road and the finishing-point of the walk.

*1 Sarn Helen Roman road*

This section of the route crosses the southern moorlands of Fforest Fawr in an unswerving, purposeful manner, its straight-as-a-die alignment betraying its origins as a Roman road. Its construction linked the Roman forts at Neath (Nidum) and Coelbren with the key stronghold of Y Gaer just west of Brecon. When the Romans invaded Wales in force in AD 74, they knew that their conquest depended on good communications, so they built Sarn Helen (Helen's Cause-way), a long-distance route linking South and North Wales.

*2 Pwll-y-Rhyd*

This spectacular formation, located just downstream from the bridge, is a gigantic swallow-hole which gobbles up the whole of the Nedd after the rains. The river pours into this deep limestone fissure, disappearing underground for a short distance to re-emerge at White Lady Cave. In dry conditions, what water there is in the river will have already disappeared down swallow-holes and fissures upstream from Pwll-y-Rhyd, leaving a dry river-bed.

*3 Maen Madoc*

This slender 9-ft-high (2.7 m) stone stands on a windy ridge beside Sarn Helen. It is a fascinating reflection of the way in which native and invading cultures inevitably mix as well as clash. Originally, it was probably a plain standing stone of Celtic origin. After the Roman occupation, it was inscribed with the message, in Latin, '(The stone) of Dervacus, son of Justus. He lies here.'

# 1.5

# GARN GOCH IRON AGE HILLFORT

STARTING AND FINISHING
POINT
Rough verge parking on unfenced
minor road leading to Crug Glas Farm
and Garn Goch fort (Outdoor Leisure
Sheet 12/684242)
LENGTH
4½ miles (7 km)
ASCENT
800 ft (240 m)

Suitable for all the family, this peaceful and quiet walk into ancient history follows old farm tracks through remote fields and woodland up to the fine view-point afforded by Trichrug Hill. The return journey down an old road crosses the impressive yet little-known Iron Age hillfort of Garn Goch, which is situated on a bracken-covered hilltop above the Tywi Valley, close to the tiny hamlet of Bethlehem (famous for its Christmas postmark).

## ROUTE DESCRIPTION (Map 6)

Walk back down the narrow farm road to the Garn Goch signpost, turn L, go up the hill, and turn L again at the sign to Trap. Continue for ½ mile (800 m) along the tarmac road, passing Cwm-du Cottage, to reach a gate and public path on the left, just before a small stream which runs under the road. Go through the gate, follow the stream along a well-worn track for 300 yards (275 m) and then turn half L across the field to reach another gate.

Cross the rough pasture land ahead, following an old hedge line and a series of stiles along the public right-of-way to a sharp corner of the dense conifer plantation. Continue walking up a sunken trackway beside the forest boundary to reach Carreglwyd Farm *(1)*. A small arboretum of decorative conifers was planted thirty years ago on the forest edge by the Forestry Commission as a garden for the benefit of the farming family. Sadly, the nineteenth-century farmhouse has fallen into ruin and the arboretum is left untended.

Look behind the fallen tree and tangled hedge for a stile onto the farm track. Go through the rickety forest gate, then turn immediately L up a steep and narrow grassy path leading into an attractive open glade of mature larch trees. Walk uphill through bracken and long grass to find a mossy forest track overhung by larch and spruce. Turn L along this moist green tunnel, walking

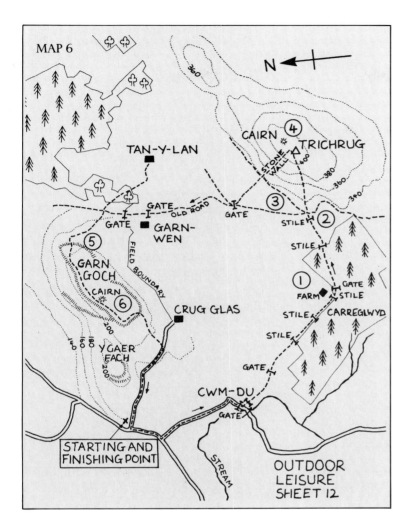

for ¼ mile (400 m) to a fence, stile, and tumbled-down drystone wall. Climb over the piled stone and continue straight across the field ahead, walking along an old raised hedge-bank with a very wet area of marshy ground (2) on your right to a further stile and fence on the far side, just beyond a stream.

Walk on 25 yards (20 m) to join the Garn-wen road (3), an ancient grassy track that winds around the base of the hill. The rock-strewn pasture ahead is called Trichrug and is an area of wild upland grazing surmounted by a large Bronze Age cairn. Climb straight up Trichrug, heading for the highest point, to gain fine views (4) in all directions. The view southward reveals the steep mountain walls and sweeping extent of the Carmarthen Fans, while that to the north across Garn Goch Hill looks into the very heart of Wales toward the distant line of the Cambrian Mountains.

Descend from Trichrug in a north-westerly direction,

walking steeply downhill along the straight line of drystone wall
to the very bottom. Here you rejoin the Garn-wen road where
it passes through a gate into the enclosed farmland. Turn sharp
L just inside the gate and follow the old road down through the
fields for ½ mile (800 m) past a small ruined barn to reach a
further gate just above Garn-wen Farm. Where the path is very
wet walk along the field edge, rejoining the track lower down.
Bear R past Garn-wen along the farm lane to a further gate onto
a narrow tarmac road. The unfenced heath ahead is part of the
Garn Goch common, an open area of rough grazing land owned
by the National Park.

Continue for 200 yards (180 m) to a junction, where a track
joins the tarmac road from the R. Turn half L onto the heathland
and walk uphill, following an indistinct path to the tumbled
stone rampart of Garn Goch fort (5) visible on the hill above.
Enter the fort by a narrow gap in the rampart. This eastern
gateway is the original main entrance and was flanked by stone
watch-towers complete with heavy wooden gates. Turn R just
inside the entrance, following a narrow path beside the piled
stone of the northern rampart. Here there are splendid views of
green fields and water meadows across the wide plain of the
river Tywi down below on your right. The large ponds beside
the Tywi are ox-bow lakes left behind when the river changed
its course.

Continue on past a large Bronze Age cairn (6) to reach the
sharp western corner of the rampart overlooking the
neighbouring hill of Y Gaer fach (small fort). This lesser
fortification is part of the Garn Goch complex and is thought to
have been built at about the same time. Walk across the stony
ground inside the west wall to find a gap and a trackway.
Descend the track, keeping half R at a junction, to join the
tarmac road. Note the holes and depressions in the stonework
above. These gaps in the rampart are the work of stone-robbers,
who removed the larger blocks of stone for building purposes
elsewhere. As Garn Goch is now a protected Ancient
Monument, the removal of any material from the site is illegal.

The starting-point of the walk is ¼ mile (400 m) along the
road to your right.

### 1 Carreglwyd Farm

Built in 1800, this redundant farmstead has met the same fate
as many other smallholdings in the area, proving too small to
survive in the modern agricultural climate. The surrounding
fields have been bought up and form part of a much larger

*The ramparts of Garn Goch from the slopes of Trichrug and Pen y Bicws*

farm nearby.

2  *Wetlands*

The farmland around Garn Goch has many boggy fields and areas of undrained wetland of no use to the farmer but of great value as haven and habitat for various wild flowers, aquatic plants, amphibians and insects. The marshland below Trichrug contains sedges and wild flowers such as ragged robin, ladies' smock and marsh marigold, species typical of damp pasture land.

3  *Garn-wen road*

This old road, fallen out of use by wheeled traffic, is still classified as an official county roadway open to the public. During the nineteenth century the area had a much larger population and this route was a main thoroughfare busy with local farm traffic and droves of cattle heading for market. The old road still remains, lapsing into decay and reminding us of a bygone age.

4  *Trichrug Hill*

A large Bronze Age cairn on top of Trichrug has been much reduced over the years for nearby stone-wall building. Looking south from the top, you see the great sweep of mountain escarpment that forms the backbone of the National Park, stretching for 50 miles (80 km) from the Black Mountain to the central Beacons and beyond. Several ancient roads cross over this mountain range, making a historical link between rural mid-Wales and the industrial valleys to the south. Looking north, the Cambrian Mountains can be seen on the horizon, providing an expansive backcloth for Garn Goch hillfort, which straddles the bracken-covered hilltop in the foreground.

5  *Garn Goch hillfort*

Garn Goch is the Y Gaer fawr (Big Fort) and central strong point of a large military complex that dominated the Tywi Valley during the late Iron Age. The heyday of Garn Goch was around 400 BC when a considerable community occupied a village and farmland on the southern slopes outside the rampart. The flat centre of the fort was the stronghold of the chieftain, and a number of large storehouses and other buildings are thought to have stood here. These warehouses at Garn Goch were a collecting point and political power-base for the control of the large trade between the upland and coastal communities.

The defences at Garn Goch were considerable, with a great stone rampart built at enormous effort, surrounding an area far too large to defend, given the very low population of the Iron Age. Stone watch-towers defended two wooden gates at the east and west ends and various other defensive works include two well-preserved sally ports on the southern side. There is no evidence of any battle being fought at Garn Goch and it seems likely that this massive fortification was largely symbolic, built to impress rather than defend. The fort was abandoned before the Romans arrived and later evidence suggests alternative use as a cattle stockade. In the Middle Ages, wooden huts or shelters were erected inside.

6 *Bronze Age cairn*

This landmark was erected long before the building of Garn Goch, for it dates back to the Bronze Age. The top of the cairn is flattened, a modification carried out in the early nineteenth century, when the Toll-Gate Breakers rallied at Garn Goch and lit a beacon on top of the cairn as the signal for simultaneous rioting and toll-gate breaking all along the Tywi Valley. These revolutionaries, also known as the Rebecca Rioters, often disguised themselves as women to avoid being stopped by the police and the military.

*The entrance to Garn Goch Iron Age fort*

# 1.6

# Carreg Cennen and River Loughor

**STARTING AND FINISHING POINT**
Carreg Cennen Castle car-park beside Castell Farm (Outdoor Leisure Sheet 12/666194)
**LENGTH**
4½ miles (7 km)
**ASCENT**
400 ft (120 m)

This attractive circular walk along agricultural lanes and footpaths is suitable for all ages and makes a great half-day out for all the family. The walk descends into the Cennen Valley along a waymarked route through field and meadow to the source of the River Loughor, then returns to Carreg Cennen along an old farm road to the foot of the castle cliff. The final mile (1.6 km) of the walk is mostly uphill through castle woodland, to reach the high limestone crag above. There are several natural and historical features along the way, the most outstanding of which is Carreg Cennen, a spectacular castle complete with dungeon and ancient cave.

## Route Description (Map 7)

From the car-park go back along the minor road, then turn L at the first junction and walk downhill into the Cennen Valley for ½ mile (800 m). Cross over a stile in the hedgerow on the R just before Pantyffynnont Cottage, then go straight down across the fields, crossing two further stiles to reach the river. Take care where the path is slippery and steep, just above the water-meadow. Cross over the river by the narrow footbridge (note the novel sheep barrier), walk on to an iron-rail gate, then go uphill along the public path to reach Llwyn-bedw farm. Turn R and follow the stony farm track for ½ mile (800 m) through fields and rough grazing land to ford a stream, then carry on uphill to a junction just beyond a small cattle-grid. Turn L through the open gateway and follow the approximate track to reach a stream and a stone-flag bridge. Look back along the stream's course for a view across fields and woodland to the castle cliff. A solitary heron can often be seen flapping along the Cennen Valley, seeking fishing grounds in the marshy land below.

Walk on, crossing two stiles, then on beside a stream for ¼ mile (400 m) to reach a small enclosure of trees and a stile on

50

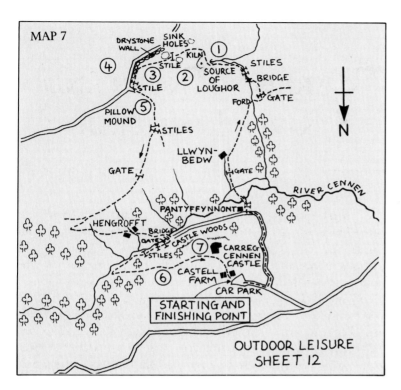

MAP 7

DRYSTONE SINK
WALL HOLES
①
KILN
STILE STILES
④ SOURCE
③ OF BRIDGE
② LOUGHOR
STILE GATE
FORD
PILLOW ⑤
MOUND
STILES
LLWYN-
BEDW
GATE
GATE
RIVER CENNEN

PANTYFFYNNONT

HENGROFFT
BRIDGE CASTLE WOODS
GATE
STILES ⑦ CARREG
CENNEN
CASTLE
⑥ CASTELL
FARM
CAR PARK

**STARTING AND
FINISHING POINT**

OUTDOOR LEISURE
SHEET 12

N

the right. This is the source of the River Loughor and the river-cave and pool can be seen from the high bank above. There is a short limestone cave system here, reaching into the depths of the hillside and only accessible to the experienced caver *(1)*. Continue along the track, bearing R past an old lime kiln with a limestone quarry behind *(2)*. The kiln was last worked around the turn of the century, producing burnt lime for local industry.

Just beyond the kiln the track disappears into open grazing land. Follow the line of the old stone wall to a stile between two large craters. These are shake holes caused by the ground collapsing into limestone caverns beneath *(3)*. Several mature trees growing in these holes indicate that they were formed some time ago.

Walk straight on to reach a drystone wall at the edge of a narrow tarmac road. Turn L and go along the line of the wall to a stile. The open land to your right is the western edge of the Black Mountain *(4)*, a vast area of wild upland stretching for many miles to the south and east.

Cross the stile, walk L along the road for 100 yards (90 m) then turn L again onto a grass track past the ancient Pillow Mounds *(5)* to a row of trees, where you can glimpse Carreg Cennen Castle in the distance. Go straight on, crossing a stile, a stream and another stile on your R into a field. Walk the length of this open pasture to a gate, a trackway and a National Park

sign at the further end. To your L is a magnificent view of the castle and tree-clad slopes of the high limestone cliff.

Follow the directed path on along the hillside, descending by the muddy track toward Hengrofft Farm in the valley below. Walk through the farmyard, then onto the minor road at a bridge across the Cennen. Turn sharp R through a gate and go on beside the river across several small meadows and stiles to join a waymarked path that climbs back half L up through the castle woodland (6) to the cliff-top above. On reaching the summit turn L to visit the castle (7) or R down the tarmac path, through Castell Farm to the car-park and your starting-point below.

1 *Limestone caves*

The limestone areas of the National Park are riddled with water-worn cave systems created by natural underground rivers and streams that descend from mountain and moorland heights above. Whole rivers are often swallowed up, disappearing into a cave or pothole, to re-emerge some distance lower down.

2 *Old lime kilns*

Limestone quarrying was once a major industry in the area and there are a number of disused kilns and quarries hidden away amid the farmland. Limestone had various uses in the local economy, among them providing stone for barns and houses, limestone dust for making cement and render, and, when burnt in kilns, agricultural quick-lime. The nearby quarries on top of the Black Mountain once employed hundreds of local people, making limestone products for both farming and industry.

3 *Shake holes*

Pits, craters and holes in the ground appear everywhere in limestone country and are caused by a collapse of the millstone-grit layer into the water-eroded caves of the carboniferous limestone below. Shake holes can be enormous, and it is not unkown for whole buildings to disappear swallowed up by the earth.

4 *The Black Mountain*

Designated as a Remote Area and a Site of Special Scientific Interest, the Black Mountain is one of the last truly wild areas of countryside left in Britain and has several fascinating geographical and geological features. These include extensive limestone pavements on the summit, crevasses which contain alpine plants and the great knife-edged Fan Hir ridge which has been sculpted by glaciation.

*Dramatic Carreg Cennen Castle, perched on its limestone crag*

5  *Pillow Mounds*

The area of hummocky land known as the Pillow Mounds is thought to be a Bronze Age burial site, dating from about 3000 BC. However, a less romantic explanation suggests that the long low mounds are Victorian rabbit warrens, created in the late nineteenth century as part of the local industry of breeding rabbits for meat.

6  *Castle Woodland*

The steep hillside of Carreg Cennen is clad with self-seeded oak woodland. Over the years many good trees have fallen owing to the steep, unstable ground and others have died of disease and old age. Because of constant grazing by sheep, there are no saplings to replace the declining tree stock and it seems that the woodland of Carreg Cennen is doomed to disappear unless a management scheme can be agreed.

7  *Carreg Cennen Castle*

Built on a natural 300-ft (90 m) limestone crag above the Cennen Valley, the main structure and defences of the castle were erected during the great thirteenth-century building boom, under the victorious English king, Edward I. Many castles were built all over Wales to consolidate English rule and Carreg Cennen was a key stronghold in the local area of South Wales. The Earl of Hereford and John Gifford constructed most of the major fortifications, adding various towers and employing defensive ideas borrowed from the great castles of Europe.

The castle has passed through several sieges and periods of destruction, having been attacked and taken by various Welsh and English armies over the centuries. Its captors include Llywelyn the Prince of Wales and the last great Welsh national leader, Owain Glyndŵr. The castle was partly demolished in 1462 to render it unusable by local bandits, who plagued the countryside at that time.

Carreg Cennen is one of the great historic spectacles of Wales. Its location—it teeters on a sheer cliff in the foothills of the Black Mountain—is unforgettable. There is even spectacle beneath the ground here. A narrow passageway cut into the cliff leads to a cave-like dungeon and a natural tunnel, where the bones of four Stone Age skeletons (two adults and two children) were discovered. A torch and guide-book are available from Castell Farm tea-shop.

*Castell Farm, in the shadow of Carreg Cennen*

# THE SUGAR LOAF

STARTING AND FINISHING
POINT
Car-park on the southern approach to
the summit, signposted off the A40
on the western outskirts of
Abergavenny (Outdoor Leisure Sheet
13/268167)
LENGTH
4 miles (6.5 km)
ASCENT
825 ft (250 m)

This is a difficult walk to categorize. On the face of it, it seems better off among the Grade 1 routes. However, its Grade 2 classification is earned by the complexities of route-finding on this mountain. Not that you will fail to find any well-defined paths to the top of this bulky peak, which dominates the Usk Valley around Abergavenny. On the contrary, the problem comes from the wealth of footpaths along the flanks of the Sugar Loaf's grassy, open uplands. Footpaths, trackways, sheep-paths and pony-trekking trails (not all of them marked on the 1:50 000 OS map) criss-cross and interlink, creating a confusing series of junctions and a maze of options.

'I was told to follow the path to the summit; but which path?' is the question commonly asked by puzzled walkers on the Sugar Loaf. On a clear day, the problem is much less acute; with the summit in view, you will get to the top, probably on your chosen route. But on a misty day, navigation is much more difficult among this spider's web of trackways.

Scenically, this walk is outstandingly attractive. The views are spectacular even from the car-park at the starting-point, and they get better and better all the way to the summit.

## ROUTE DESCRIPTION (Map 8)

From the car-park *(1)*, take the path past the National Trust plinth for the summit. The grassy flanks of the Sugar Loaf are eroded here to reveal the distinctive sandy-red soils of the Brecon Beacons' old red sandstone rocks. After just over ⅓ mile (0.5 km) the path joins a tumbledown drystone wall (on the L). At this point, there is a fork in the path. Bear L along the grassy track that runs close to the wall (the first of the many confusing junctions referred to earlier).

For the next ⅓ mile (0.5 km), stay on the path as it follows the drystone wall. At the point along the path where the wall begins to drop gently down the hillside, keep straight on along the main footpath (a secondary path follows the wall downhill). From here, the path is well defined as it cuts a grassy corridor

*Overleaf: There are huge vistas in all directions from the Sugar Loaf summit*

through the ferns and bracken.

Just over ⅓ mile (0.5 km) after the path has left the drystone wall, you will reach a meeting of tracks, at the point where the route begins to ascend to the summit (until now, the path has been quite level). If you abide by the OS map here you turn R, and within 150 yards (140 m) turn L at a low earth bank and gully running up the mountainside. You can, in effect, go straight on instead of turning R and come to the earth bank a little farther up the slope—see 'cross-path' on the map.

On the approach to the summit, the bank peters out and the path becomes less well marked as it weaves its way among a scattering of boulders and outcropping rocks. The Sugar Loaf summit *(2)* is a very popular place on a clear day, and even in misty conditions attracts a fair share of enthusiasts who have to make do with picturing the view in their mind's eye.

Descend from the summit in a south-easterly direction (*not* by the stone staircase which connects with a path leading north-east). The route is initially indeterminate as it picks its way down a steep slope among the heather and the boulders, though on a clear day you should be able to see the intended path farther down the slope. The first real landmark is the mossy, boggy hollow (on the L) which is the source of a spring.

The path, which follows the line of the spring as it flows down a deep gully, becomes well defined as it cuts through the ferns, crossing the stream in its lower reaches. Just under ¼ mile (0.4 km) after the stream crossing, turn back half R at a cross-path to follow a wide, grassy track which skirts the side of the mountain. Go straight on at the next cross-path, and within ¼ mile (0.4 km) bear half L at the junction, walking in a south-westerly direction.

At the next junction, a wide, open meeting of the ways, go straight on. Within ¼ mile (0.4 km), go straight on again at another little cross-path and shortly rejoin the outward leg of the route (by the drystone wall) to retrace your steps to the car-park.

*1 View-point at car-park*

Many visitors are attracted to this wonderfully located car-park, which stands at 1132 ft (345 m) on Mynydd Llanwenarth on the southern and western shoulders of the Sugar Loaf. The land drops away abruptly into the Usk Valley, the river snaking in a lazy loop directly below. The Automobile Association has erected here an orientation pillar which identifies many landmarks, including the 1833-ft (560 m) summit of Blorenge directly opposite, the 1735-ft (530 m) Mynydd Llangatwg 4½ miles (7 km) away, and the 2504-ft

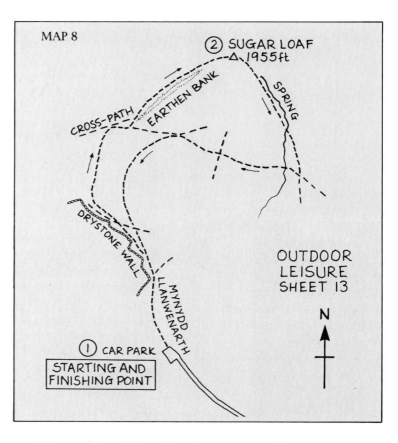

MAP 8

② SUGAR LOAF
△ 1955ft

CROSS-PATH  EARTHEN BANK  SPRING

DRYSTONE WALL

MYNYDD LLANWENARTH

OUTDOOR
LEISURE
SHEET 13

N

① CAR PARK
STARTING AND
FINISHING POINT

*The view eastwards to Ysgyryd Fawr (The Skirrid) from the Sugar Loaf*

(760 m) peak of Waen-Rhyd (or Waen-rydd), 12½ miles (20 km) distant.

2  *Sugar Loaf summit*

The views from here are, of course, even better. The north-western face, shaped like the prow of a ship, looks out across the pastoral Usk Valley towards the heart of the National Park, while to the north and north-east the landscape is dominated by the Black Mountains, which run along the Wales–England border. A geologically interesting landmark can be seen 4 miles (6.5 km) to the north-west. This is the peak of Pen Cerrig-calch (2302 ft/700 m), a limestone outcrop surrounded by sandstones. It is the isolated, final remnant of the band of carboniferous limestone rocks which are found along the southern rim of the National Park, *calch* being the Welsh for lime.

The horizontal slabs of rock on the summit of the Sugar Loaf have proved irresistible to graffiti artists for some time. Carefully carved signatures appear everywhere, together with dates going back to the turn of the century. The Sugar Loaf was presented to the National Trust in 1936, partly in commemoration of the Jubilee of King George V.

# ACROSS THE CARMARTHEN FANS

STARTING AND FINISHING
POINT
Brest Cwm Llwyd car-park on minor
road off the A4069 (Outdoor Leisure
Sheet 12/708194)
LENGTH
5½ miles (9 km)
ASCENT
700 ft (210 m)

Ancient trackways and roads of various periods traverse the mountain wilderness of the Carmarthen Fans. This walk follows a nineteenth-century carriage road, once the main route for horse-drawn traffic between Gwynfe and Brynaman. The route climbs a series of gently graded and well-built terraces to the summit of tussocky moorland above, then follows a straight line across the high plateaux to reach a miners' track and the A4069 on the southern side. The return journey across limestone country visits an old kiln and a silica-sand quarry below the summit of Foel Fawr.

## ROUTE DESCRIPTION (Map 9)

Cross over the tarmac road from the small car-park and join the broad grassy track of the old road. Keep R at the first junction and continue on to the top of the mountain. The track disappears halfway up at an area of boggy ground. To avoid getting lost, walk on in a straight line, to rediscover the path after a few hundred yards. Close to the summit the route is clearly marked by rows of piled stones which indicate the borders of a broad avenue *(1)* extending for ½ mile (800 m) across the flat mountain top. Go on to where the stone avenue ends, then strike out slightly L and uphill to reach the south side of the mountain at Garreg fraith. The line of the A4069 is visible below. Look directly south for a magnificent view of the South Wales coast and the hills of North Devon beyond. A few hundred yards in front is an old quarry track. Follow this grassy path downhill to just above the A4069. The rugged landscape ahead is the remote southern side *(2)* of the Black Mountain, stretching for many miles eastward.

Turn L and follow the sheep tracks running parallel with the road for about 1 mile (1.6 km) to reach some sandpits and a car-park and toilets opposite. The narrow road to the L of the toilets leads to Rhiw Wen stone quarries and kilns *(3)*, an old industrial

*Overleaf: Wild, inhospitable moorland
in the brooding Black Mountain*

site last worked during the 1930s. Cross over the A4069 and follow the quarry road for ¼ mile (400 m) to explore the kilns and quarries. Return by the same route, cross back over the A4069 and ascend the hill to the R of the disused sandpits *(4)*, looking for a stone cairn on the summit of Pen Rhiw-ddu. From this vantage point there are fine views *(5)* of the surrounding landscape. Walk downhill from the cairn in a north-westerly direction, keeping the hairpin bend on your R and carefully crossing the steep scree of loose boulders. On reaching an old quarry track, turn L and continue in a north-westerly direction, keeping the minor road in sight for ½ mile (800 m). Join the road, turn L and walk back to your starting-point.

### 1 The Old Road

The piled stones marking the edge of the road were an aid to navigation across the barren mountain and helped to keep large droves of sheep and cattle on course. Elderly people in the nearby village of Gwynfe recall several names for this old route, including 'Roman road'. These names suggest much earlier origins than those of a preacher's path, for the latter use goes back only to the days of the Methodist Revival, when travelling lay-preachers would visit several chapels on a Sunday, receiving a fee at each for their uplifting sermon. The most unusual name for this old road is the 'cinema path', an unlikely nickname dating from the 1930s, when the Sunday outing for non-chapelgoers was a walk or ride over the mountain to the cinema at Brynaman. In addition to the excitement of the latest feature film, cinema-goers would enjoy panoramic views of mid-Wales to the north and, on reaching the summit, a breathtaking landscape of the South Wales coast.

### 2 The southern side

The geology of this southern side is largely carboniferous limestone with millstone grit above. There can be seen numerous shake holes, where the grit layer has collapsed into water-eroded limestone caves beneath the surface. The whole southern face of the mountain is designated a Remote Wilderness Area by the National Park Authority and no development of any kind is permitted. The Remote Area is one of the last truly wild places in Britain, possessing species of rare plant life and unusual geological and geographical formations found only in this part of Wales.

### 3 Limestone quarries and kilns

The lime kilns and quarries at Rhiw Wen were once a significant industry employing a sizeable local workforce. Limestone extracted from the quarries was crushed, loaded into the tops of kilns and fired to a high temperature, to turn it into quick-lime.

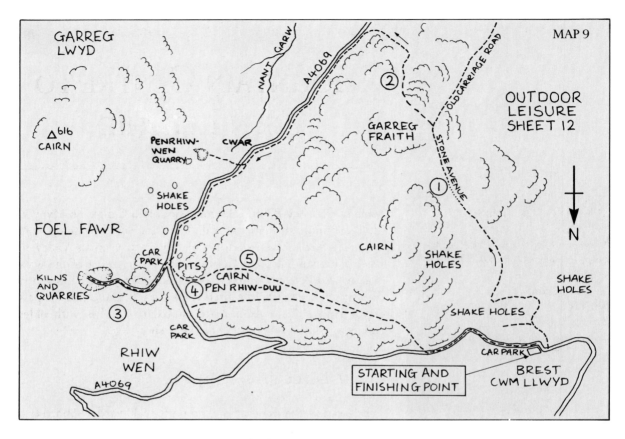

The burnt lime was used by local farmers for spreading on the fields and by builders for making cement and render. Working conditions at Foel Fawr during the winter must have been appalling as the quarries are exposed to the full force of the weather on this north-facing mountain.

*4 Sandpits*

These old pits are the remains of silica-sand quarries last worked during the nineteenth century. The old Penwyllt Brickworks at Craig-y-nos used silica-sand for the making of high-vitreous oven bricks right up to the end of the 1930s.

*5 The surrounding landscape*

A good length of the Carmarthen Fans can be seen from Pen Rhiw-ddu. To the east is the main summit and cliff face of Bannau Sir Gaer, with the long knife-edged ridge of the Fan Hir escarpment behind. Looking west along the tops, you can see a number of summits with a Bronze Age cairn on each. These ancient monuments are built on almost every hilltop and form a continuous unbroken chain across the National Park.

On the horizon to the north are the Cambrian Mountains, a great area of deserted upland that seems to march up through the centre of Wales to Snowdonia.

# MOUNTAIN CENTRE TO CEFN LLECHID

**STARTING AND FINISHING POINT**
Mountain Centre car-park (Outdoor Leisure Sheet 11/976263)
**LENGTH**
8 miles (13 km)
**ASCENT**
225 ft (70 m)

Starting from the Brecon Beacons Mountain Centre on Mynydd Illtyd common, this circular walk follows a varied route through low-lying farm- and woodland of the Cwm Camlais Valley to reach the open hilltop of Cefn Llechid. A large part of the walk is along old drovers' roads, crossing long stretches of deserted countryside by these little-used trackways. Waymarked for part of the route, this walk is better suited to families with older children, as it is rather long for very short legs.

## ROUTE DESCRIPTION (Maps 10, 11)

Turn L out of the car-park and go on for 500 yards (450 m) to a junction. Go straight on, following a rutted trackway beside the conifers, then on for 1 mile (1.6 km) following the fence line to a junction at Traeth Bach marshland (there is a group of farm buildings visible 500 yards/450 m ahead).

Turn R just before the marsh and go on across open common, following the main track north-west for a further mile (1.6 km) to reach a tarmac road. This common land is home for many species of wild birds, including redshanks, lapwings, snipe, skylarks, and other birds of the marshes and moorland.

On reaching the hard road, cross over the tarmac and go straight on along the broad grassy way ahead. This drovers' road *(1)*, dating from the eighteenth century, was once a main thoroughfare for great herds of Welsh cattle moving east to the English markets. Follow this old road for 1½ miles (2.5 km) along the east side of the Cwm Camlais Valley, crossing a series of gates and stiles. After ½ mile (400 m) you will come to an interesting old stone wall *(2)* on the L, just before a fence across the path. Turn R, then L through the gate and continue along the field edge, rejoining the old road after a few hundred yards. The path stops at Cwm Camlais wood. Turn L and follow the fence along to cross over a gate, then skirt along the field edge past several fallen trees, ignoring two further gates, to reach a

*Looking across Cefn Llechid*

sunken lane at the field corner.

The deep gorge of the Cwm Camlais *fach* (small) is down below to the right. The woodland here contains a variety of trees including ash, hazel, rowan and several splendid old oaks along the edge of the sunken lane. Go on down the lane for ¼ mile (400 m), ducking under low branches to join a used agricultural track, then onto a ford at the junction of the two rivers. A wooden footbridge crossing the Cwm Camlais gives easy passage for walkers, as well as a good view of small waterfalls and rocks in the rushing stream. The Cwm Camlais *fawr* (big) and *fach* meet here beneath the bridge.

Go on along the well-made track to reach the working farm of Cwm-Camlais-uchaf. Walk through the farmyard, being careful to close both gates behind you and turn L onto a tarmac road. Go on for ¼ mile (400 m), keeping R at two junctions, to climb a steep hill between high hedgerows. Look for a stile and waymark on the L up a narrow grassy lane. This is the way up to Cefn Llechid, a small area of open hill land owned by the National Park Authority. The narrow path between old overgrown hedges leads to two stiles and an open field. Bear R and go on up the overgrown lane to a gate leading out onto the open hill.

Cefn Llechid stretching for ½ mile (800 m) to the south-west is good for views *(3)* of the surrounding countryside. Follow the broad green path between the bracken, crossing over Cefn Llechid to find a pond and marsh on the far side.

Walk half L from the pond, skirting around the L side of the small hill, to find a stile and lane leading directly south down through the fields. This is another old drovers' road, easily identified by its broadness and the low stone walls on either side. Go on for 1 mile (1.6 km), crossing a series of stiles to reach a tarmac road. There are several species of wild flower to be seen along the way, including mauve-coloured scabious, yellow hawkweed, lady's slipper and various types of clover.

The drovers' path emerges onto a minor road at a junction with the A4215. Do not stray along the main road but turn L and follow the narrow lane for ¾ mile (1.2 km). Keep R at the junction beside Blaen-Camlais-fawr farm, cross over the bridge, and walk on up the steep hill to a sharp L-hand bend. Two hundred yards (180 m) on, just before Neuadd Cwmcamlais, turn R up a steep, stony track, walking straight uphill to rejoin the drovers' road above. Turn R and go on to the tarmac road at the edge of Mynydd Illtyd common.

To return to your starting-point, turn L, following the course of the road across open land toward Llanilltyd Farm *(4)*, then walk along the tarmac back to the Mountain Centre.

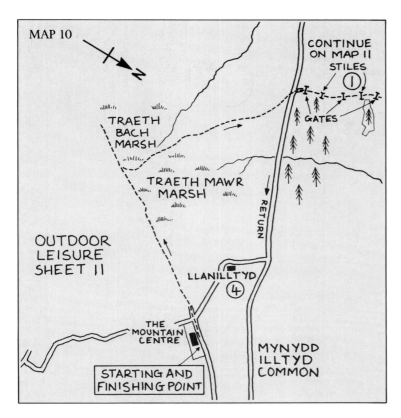

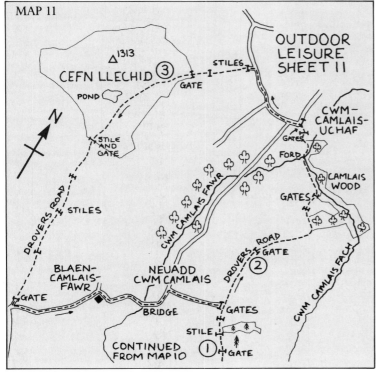

1 *Drovers' roads*

Wales was once the 'Wild West' of Britain, with huge herds of Welsh black cattle moving along drovers' roads from the fields of Carmarthenshire eastward to England. Drove roads followed old ways across the remote hills, thus avoiding towns, villages and expensive tolls along the turnpike roads. The drovers, a special breed of freebooting gentlemen, would negotiate a price with local farmers along the route for driving their stock to distant markets in Hereford and Gloucester. During the journey, herds would grow to many thousands of beasts.

2 *Old stone walls*

The old road here is edged with upright stones. These were originally erected to direct and contain the herds, preventing animals spilling over into surrounding countryside. The large blocks of stone often served as foundations for later horizontal stone-wall building and several good examples can be seen along the walk.

3 *Views from Cefn Llechid*

When you look south-east, the Brecon Beacons loom large on the skyline, with worn tracks to be seen leading up to the summit of Corn Du. Pen y Fan, the highest point, measures 2906 ft (886 m) and stands just to the left behind Corn Du. Cwm Llwch is farther left, forming a great hollow amphitheatre below the high ridges of Craig Cwm Llwch and Pen Milan.

Directly south from Cefn Llechid and closer to hand is Fan Frynych, measuring 2063 ft (630 m), and farther right are the high wastes of Fforest Fawr, the 'Great Forest', with the beautiful and wild Senni Valley cutting deeply into the hills. Great bare green slopes, turning to gold in autumn, are the signature of the Beacons. These hills are constantly changing colour and the view from this point varies tremendously with the passage of the months.

4 *Llanilltyd*

The common takes its name from Saint Illtyd, the visionary who established a small monastery close to the site of Llanilltyd Farm. Illtyd was a sixth-century monk who lived during the golden age of the independent Celtic Church. He was a teacher and visionary with extraordinary powers, who commanded a great following of men and women devoted to the religious life. His contemporaries and students include such figures as David, Teilo, Cadog, Paulinus and other famous saints of the post-Roman age. Saint Illtyd is said to be buried on the common close to the original church, but his remains have yet to be discovered.

# Y Pigwn Roman Camp

Roadside parking on north side of
Usk Reservoir, 250 yards (225 m)
beyond keeper's house (Outdoor
Leisure Sheet 12/828292)
LENGTH
5½ miles (9 km)
ASCENT
360 ft (110 m)

The beautiful and deserted moorland of Mynydd Bach Trecastell
is a place of silence and solitude. There are fine views of the
Carmarthen Fans from Y Pigwn marching camp and a wealth of
historical remains to be seen, including the Roman gold route
and several Bronze Age stones.

Suitable for families with older children, this walk starts at
the Usk Reservoir dam and ascends through the conifer forest
of Glasfynydd to join the Roman road on the hills above. The
return journey follows the old road down to Hafod Fawr, then
back to the forest and reservoir by farm track, across the hills
and marshland of Waun ddu. You will need a compass for
navigation across the hill land.

## Route Description (Map 12)

Climb over the stile and go up the hard road into the forest,
turning R at the first junction along a muddy forest path, then
on for ½ mile (800 m) uphill through dense plantations of
spruce and larch. You will come to a hard road and a forestry
turning circle. Bear R along the grassy track to find and follow a
small waymarker post pointing R down through the larch trees
to a stile and rushing stream at the forest boundary. Climb up
the steep bank ahead onto the wide, open moorland of Mynydd
Bach Trecastell. These green, rolling hills are owned by the
National Park Authority and form a small corner of the huge
Black Mountain Estate. Walk on almost due north across the
moorland toward Y Pigwn and the Roman road, following a
bearing of 10° magnetic for 1 mile (1.6 km). The ground ahead
is very boggy in places. For easy passage keep to the slightly
higher ground where the grass grows, avoiding wet areas of dark
reed and moss.

The Roman camp, visible as a series of irregular bumps and
mounds on the horizon ahead, straddles the hillside above the
line of the Roman road *(1)*, which appears as a narrow, well-
defined track stretching both east and west. As you look east, a
small Bronze Age cairn can be seen just to the L of the road.

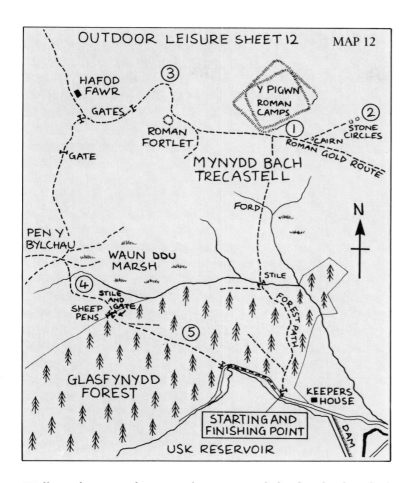

*The Usk Reservoir*

Walk to the cairn then straight on toward the farmland to find two small Bronze Age stone circles *(2)*.

Return by the same route and walk west along the Roman road for ½ mile (800 m) past several pools of standing water to reach a junction in a hollow next to the Roman fortlet. Bear R, following the main route, and continue to the edge of the hill overlooking the fields and woods of the farmland *(3)* below. Go on down the old road to reach a gate in the field boundary, then on to a junction at a further gate just beyond a stream crossing the road. The ancient farm of Hafod Fawr can be seen a short distance ahead. Turn L through the gate and follow the public path back up to the mountain boundary. Walk on across the open hillside for ½ mile (800 m), following the rough track at first, then using a compass bearing of 190° magnetic where the path disappears, to reach a crossroads on the far side of the hill at Pen y Bylchau.

Several old roads converge at this ancient meeting of the ways. Follow the well-defined track leading approximately south toward Sheep Pens (marked on OS Outdoor Leisure map) at the edge of the conifer forest. You will cross part of Waun Ddu *(4)*, an area of treacherous marshland where sheep and horses have been known to disappear. Do not stray from the well-defined road. Go through the forest gate, bear slightly R at the first junction, then straight on by forest track *(5)* for ½ mile (800 m) downhill, to reach the tarmac perimeter road at the edge of the reservoir. Turn L and walk for ¼ mile (400 m) along the road back to your starting-point.

*1 Roman road and Y Pigwn camp*

This ancient track across the hills, once the main road into West Wales, was used as a regular thoroughfare right up to the Victorian period. The Romans exported gold from the Welsh hills and this road was their route east from the Imperial Mines at nearby Dolaucothi. Heavy fortifications built along the route helped to defend the gold convoy. Y Pigwn camp and the nearby fortlet were part of these defences, serving as overnight stopping-points for both troops and baggage trains marching east, with ore bound for London and ultimately the Imperial Mint at Lyons.

In the nineteenth century the road was used as a carriage route and fast stagecoaches from Gloucester and London trotted at a steady 10 mph (16 km/h) across this high moorland. Frequent changes of horse were necessary and staging-posts were set up along the route. A temporary stable called the Black Cock Inn was erected next to the Roman camp. It closed around 1840, when the Black Cock disappeared with the demise of the stagecoach service.

*2 Bronze Age remains*

A short distance east of Y Pigwn are two Bronze Age stone circles and a low burial cairn. These remains date from about 2000 BC, when small farming communities established huts and field systems on the high moorland during the warm post-glacial period. The term Bronze Age is misleading because the metal was hardly available for general use. These early farmers were more likely to be using tools from the earlier Stone Age technology.

*3 The farming landscape*

The field and woodland to the north is the farming area of Myddfai. This countryside has remained largely unchanged since Victorian times and has become increasingly wooded over the years. This is partly caused by old hedges growing up into substantial rows of trees and by a gradual filling out of the wooded slopes and gorges.

*Cwm y Cadno, on the route just west of the Roman camp of Y Pigwn*

4 *The marshland*

Waun Ddu is an area of upland peat bog at the base of Mynydd Myddfai. This wetland gathers water from numerous underground streams descending from the surrounding hills, and serves as a catchment area for the nearby Usk Reservoir. The conifer forest was intended to slow down this water and prevent sudden surges from topping up the reservoir too quickly. This plantation has proved too successful—and ultimately counter-productive—for the trees themselves take up a large quantity of water, seriously reducing the supply.

5 *Glasfynydd Forest*

The trees of Glasfynydd Forest are entirely spruce and larch planted by the Forestry Commission in the early 1960s, shortly after the reservoir was built. These softwoods are now reaching maturity and large areas of the forest are being felled. Commercial forestry is increasingly profitable because of great demand for timber, particularly by the building and construction industries. The current world shortage of usable timber also makes this conifer forest a very valuable national asset.

*Glasfynydd Forest*

# BLAEN-Y-GLYN AND CRAIG Y FAN DDU

**STARTING AND FINISHING POINT**
Blaen-y-glyn Forestry Commission car-park, Talybont Forest (Outdoor Leisure Sheet 11/064169)
**LENGTH**
4 miles (6.5 km)
**ASCENT**
1150 ft (350 m)

Tumbling streams, cascading waterfalls and an experience of the hills are the main features of this short but steep climb up into the heights of the eastern flanks of the central Beacons. The walk starts from Talybont Forest, follows the course of the Caerfanell River past Blaen-y-glyn waterfall to reach the amphitheatre of Cerrig Edmwnt and the summit of Craig Fan. From the top there are amazing views of mountains and forest.

The return journey by forestry path descends through the conifers above an attractive ferny gorge with numerous waterfalls. This walk, although quite short, is best suited to the fairly fit as the first half is continually uphill for 2 miles (3 km), with a final very steep climb to the summit ridge.

## ROUTE DESCRIPTION (Map 13)

Walk back down the lane from the car-park, cross over the road and follow the broad forest track to the L. Go on for ¼ mile (400 m), crossing a forest track, to reach a wooden bridge across the river, just below the splendid Blaen-y-glyn waterfall *(1)*. Cross the bridge, turn L, climb up the narrow path to the top of the falls and continue on along the R side of the river. The path, boggy in places, follows the watercourse up into the hills through sparse self-seeded woodland *(2)* with ranks of conifer forest close by on your L.

After 1 mile (1.6 km) the path and stream emerge onto the open hillside. Ahead of you is the *cwm* (wooded valley) of Cerrig Edmwnt *(3)*, surrounded by the mountain walls of Craig Fan and Waun Rydd. Follow the main stream course across this tumbled landscape, keeping L at two stream junctions to reach the high waterfall tipping off Craig Fan. Scramble up the very steep slope to the L of the waterfall in easy stages, turn L at the summit and follow the cliff-top path to the head of Craig y Fan Ddu. The rolling hills to your L are the eastern headlands of the old red sandstone escarpment *(4)* and farther to the R you will

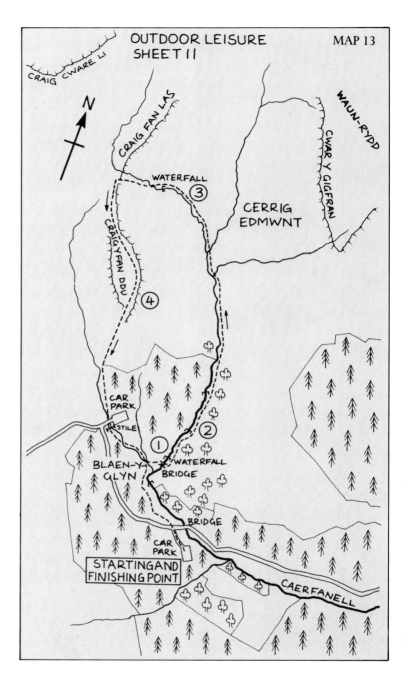

*Opposite: The emptiness of the Black Mountain from Craig y Fan Ddu*

see Talybont Valley and Forest.

Descend the head of the fan by a well-worn path leading down to the forest boundary fence, then on downhill to meet a hard track and a Forestry Commission car-park. Turn R along the rough road and look for a stile into the forest on the L, just before the tarmac road. Walk down this narrow forest path, crossing the stream above the first large waterfall, then on down

*View from the summit of Craig y Fan Ddu*

a steep, waymarked route through dense conifers to rejoin the broad forest track in the valley below. Turn R and return to your starting-point at the forestry car-park.

1  *Blaen-y-glyn waterfall*
During summer months this popular picnic spot can be quite busy, with bathers cooling off under the falls or swimming in deep pools below the footbridge. In the winter Blaen-y-glyn waterfall often freezes solid, to resemble a huge multi-tiered wedding cake surrounded by gigantic ice stalactites hanging from the grotto walls.

2  *Woodland*
Self-seeded sessile oaks grow on the R bank of the Caerfanell stream. These trees are survivors of the original native oak woodland that once filled all the valleys and clad the lower slopes of the Welsh hills. Close-packed conifers have now replaced the ancient trees, casting a gloomy, sterile shadow where the wholesome ecology of broad-leaf woodland once flourished.

However, the Talybont Forest is not entirely unattractive, efforts having been made to mix bands of larch with the inevitable spruce. Looking back down the valley during autumn reveals a colourful sight of gold and green stripes.

3  *Cerrig Edmwnt*
The great *cwm* of Cerrig Edmwnt is a glacial landscape shaped by rivers of ice descending from the heights above. The high banks and sharp-edged walls above the stream courses were pushed, scoured and cut by small glaciers, sculpting the terrain and pushing up hillocks of rock and soil. Numerous streams descending from the heights above have deepened these glacial channels and, lower down where the water gathers pace, have cut out the deep rocky gorge and waterfalls of Blaen-y-glyn.

4  *The surrounding hills*
Craig y Fan Ddu is one of the several mountain headlands that tower above the Talybont Valley. These steep escarpments are part of the great old red sandstone ridge that extends for 50 miles (80 km) westward and forms the mountain backbone of the National Park. The tops of the fans are covered in blanket peat bog, eroded in parts to form large peat hags. These weird sculptures stand up like grassy islands amid swampy seas of sterile black peat.

# HAY BLUFF AND GOSPEL PASS

**STARTING AND FINISHING POINT**
Small car-park next to a standing stone on Hay common (Outdoor Leisure Sheet 13/239374)
**LENGTH**
8 miles (13 km)
**ASCENT**
825 ft (250 m)

This circular walk around the Hay Bluff escarpment makes an excellent afternoon and evening stroll suitable for most walkers of average ability. The first mile (1.6 km) of the walk, straight up to the Bluff summit, is extremely steep but, once achieved, the remainder and majority of the route is easy going, with one steep descent down on to Rhiw Wen common.

## ROUTE DESCRIPTION (Map 14)

Cross over the road from the car-park and walk straight ahead, across the gorse-covered common, toward the summit of Hay Bluff. You will soon be labouring uphill, climbing the steep foothill in front of the main summit. Frequent short halts may be advisable to catch breath and admire the panorama of woods and fields below. Head towards the left edge of the bluff to find a narrow sheep-path, then go straight up for the final assault. On cresting the ridge, go on across the bilberry moor to the white OS obelisk, then bear R to follow a well-worn path along the top of the escarpment. Leave this main track after 100 yards (90 m) bearing R to find a narrow path close to the edge, then on along the length of Ffynnon y Parc for 1 mile (1.6 km) to reach the tarmac road at Gospel Pass.

Look north-west across the Wye Valley for a fine view into mid-Wales, while down below, close to your feet, are the rolling woodland and fields of Wenallt and Tregoyd common. The flat-topped highlands around the Hay Bluff escarpment have suffered severe erosion in places, largely due to pony-trekking (1) and the continuous passage of sheep.

The narrow Gospel Pass is part of an ancient high-level route (2) for travellers between Abergavenny and Hay-on-Wye. The view south from the top of the pass looks down a rugged, steep-sided valley toward Capel-y-ffin and Llanthony. This is the head of the Vale of Ewyas, a remote area of border country steeped in history and legend.

Cross the single-track road at Gospel Pass and go on along the worn path ahead, climbing uphill for 1 mile (1.6 km) towards the Twmpa. You will reach two walkers' cairns, one on either side, and a third cairn at the summit, marked with paint. Go on past this last cairn, following the track toward Rhiw Wen, a deep gash in the escarpment visible ½ mile (800 m) ahead. The moorland landscape in front and to your L reveals the remote nature of this high borderland *(3)*, a formidable mountain barrier between Wales and England.

Turn back half R at Rhiw Wen and go down the steep track toward the farmland. The bare cliff-face on your left is a good example of local geology *(4)*, revealing strata lines of the old red sandstone. Walk on downhill, following the worn path across two streams, to reach a small group of mature larch trees visible ahead, then straight on to the edge of the farmland below. A watercourse crosses the valley bottom and a very wide track follows the boundary fence. Turn R along this established trekking route.

Look back across the wild common land for a fine view of the hills. The northern heads of the Black Mountains form an impressive range, stretching away to the west into the heartland of Wales. The common in front is an area of upland grazing, dotted with may and oak trees, and viewed at its best during early June when the hawthorn blossom is in full bloom.

Follow the very worn track to where the fence ends, then on across the open land, walking toward Hay Bluff now visible ahead. To enjoy a walk across the common choose a route 50 yards (45 m) to one side of the heavily eroded path and go on for 1 mile (1.6 km), following the trekking route to the narrow tarmac road at Caemarchog. The mixed woodland here provides a delightful contrast with the bare windswept hills and includes a surprising mixture of oak, chestnut, ash and hazel. Turn R along the road, cross over two fords and continue along the tarmac for 1¼ miles (2 km) to reach once again your starting-point. The small meadows and woodland to the L of the road are fine examples of the traditional farming landscape now fast disappearing in other parts of Britain.

*1 Pony-trekking*

Located on the border of Wales with easy access from England, the Black Mountains are under considerable pressure from recreation and tourism. Much of this activity, such as walking and touring, is relatively benign, with little or no impact on the environment. However, the development of pony-trekking as an additional source of income for farmers and landowners has led to severe erosion of the countryside,

*Ruined farmhouse below Twmpa*

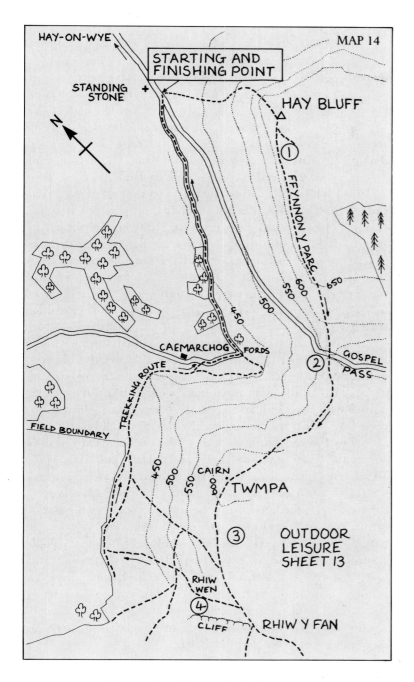

turning public rights-of-way through the farmland into muddy swamps, while tracks across the open hill become badly scarred.

*2 Gospel Pass*

This narrow gap in the hills is one of several ancient roads across the uplands and is contemporary with nearby Offa's Dyke Path. The Gospel road is much the easier route and has

remained in use throughout the centuries. The thirteenth-century canons of Llanthony Priory were regular travellers over this pass to visit their properties and fellow clerics in mid-Wales.

3 *The moorland landscape*

These mountain heights have served as a natural barrier for hundreds of years. When under attack from invading Saxons in the fifth century, the Romano-British retreated to the Black Mountains and, together with the native Welsh, defended wild Wales, the last outpost of the empire, from invasion by the Germanic tribes. The remote moorland in the centre of the mountains is largely unchanged and retains the same bleak, forbidding aspect of Roman times. This remoteness is part of the moorland's beauty and is highly valued by experienced walkers and lovers of wild country-side. To your left is the Nant Bwch Valley leading down to Capel-y-ffin and, looking south, the peak of Mynydd Llysiau can be seen on the horizon.

4 *Local geology*

Horizontal bands of hard brownstones are the very bones of the mountains, and good examples can be seen at Rhiw Wen. The steep cliff-face here has lost its grass cover, revealing the crumbling layers of rock beneath. The brownstones, solid blocks of old red sandstone, often drop out as a result of the weathering of the softer layers in between.

*Looking towards the central Beacons from the ridge below Twmpa*

# LLANTHONY VALLEY AND OFFA'S DYKE PATH

STARTING AND FINISHING
POINT
Llanthony Priory car-park (Outdoor
Leisure Sheet 13/289279)
LENGTH
8½ miles (14 km)
ASCENT
1250 ft (380 m)

The Vale of Ewyas, also known as the Llanthony Valley, stretches for many miles up into the very heart of the Black Mountains. This steep-sided valley has many historical associations reaching back to the Dark Ages and the early Celtic Church, including a connection with the legendary St David, Patron Saint of Wales. The long-distance Offa's Dyke Path follows the high ridge above the valley and marks the ancient mountain boundary between England and Wales.

This walk through history starts from the thirteenth-century Llanthony Priory and ascends the steep mountain up to Offa's Dyke Path, then on along the high ridge northwards. The return journey passes The Vision Farm, the source of inspiration for Bruce Chatwin's gripping historical novel *On the Black Hill.*

The route is suitable for most walkers of average ability, and makes a good half-day out for a family with older children.

## ROUTE DESCRIPTION (Map 15)

Go back down the lane from the car-park to a stile and a gate on the R just past the farmhouse. Follow the path around the old garden wall to another stile, which leads onto the meadowland. Go on along the wide track ahead, straight across the field with the priory buildings directly behind you, to reach a stream and a waymark pointing L, with a small sign which reads 'Way to hill'. Look back toward the priory for a view of the romantic old ruins, set amid green fields, with the steep wooded hillside of Graig Ddu behind.

Cross over the waymarked stile, walk uphill to an open gate, then on up the next field, past several dead trees, to a further stile in the top L-hand corner. Go on up steeply to a small paling gate leading onto the open hillside above. Have a brief rest here to look at the view and to catch your breath for the next stage up to the ridge above. As you look south, the whole length of the magnificent Llanthony Valley is laid out below you, with a

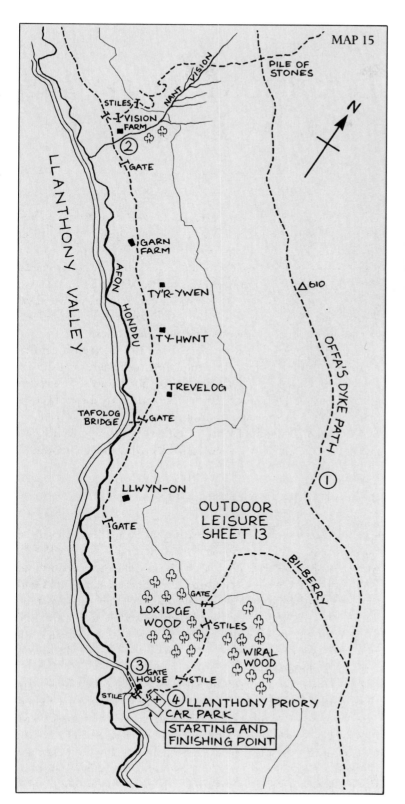

MAP 15

PILE OF STONES

NANT Y VISION

STILES

VISION FARM

②

GATE

LLANTHONY VALLEY

AFON HONDDU

GARN FARM

TY'R-YWEN

TY-HWNT

TREVELOG

TAFOLOG BRIDGE — GATE

△ 610

OFFA'S DYKE PATH

①

LLWYN-ON

GATE

OUTDOOR LEISURE SHEET 13

BILBERRY

GATE

LOXIDGE WOOD

STILES

WIRAL WOOD

③ GATE HOUSE

STILE

STILE

④ LLANTHONY PRIORY CAR PARK

STARTING AND FINISHING POINT

N

*In the hills above Llanthony*

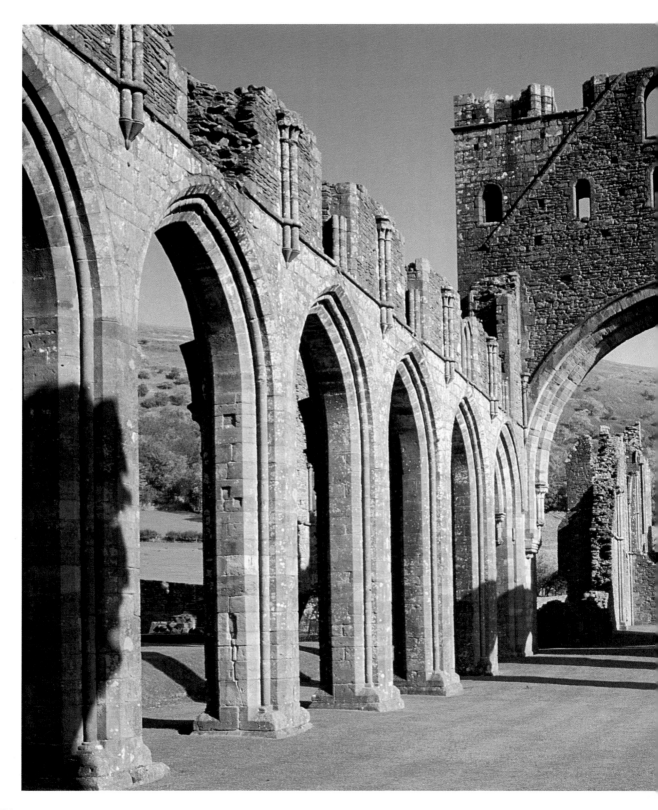

*Llanthony Priory, an evocative ruin*

fine view of the surrounding hills. Wiral Wood to your L has suffered some loss of tree cover over the years. To reverse this trend the National Park Authority has taken on a management agreement with the landowner and intends to fill gaps in the woodland canopy by planting young trees.

Go straight uphill toward a clump of thorn bushes, then bear half R, following a narrow path to a group of old box trees. These trees were once part of the front garden of a cottage. Go on uphill steeply toward the rocky summit above, to find a narrow sheep-path heading east through the bilberry, skirting around the top of Cwm Siarpal. Do not go downhill but continue up gently for 1 mile (1.6 km), toward the ridge above.

You will reach a worn track on the flat-topped summit. This is Offa's Dyke Path *(1)*. Turn L and follow the clear trackway northward toward distant Hay Bluff, walking along the Wales–England border for 3 miles (5 km). The level green fields of the Golden Valley in Herefordshire are revealed to your R and due north is the beautiful Black Hill, a high outcrop of the mountains, jutting out into England. The landscape to the L offers a complete contrast, as you look westward across the forbidding uplands of wild Wales.

You will pass several marker stones along the way and an OS obelisk (610). One mile (1.6 km) beyond this obelisk, where the track goes gently uphill, you will come to a rough crossroads, marked 'Pile of Stones' on the map. Turn L along a faint narrow path, walking down the hillside toward The Vision Farm *(2)* in the valley below. The ground is marshy in places and very steep where the Nant Vision plunges down the rocky gorge. Walk downhill to the R of the *nant* (stream), following the public path to the field boundary. Turn R at the boundary, and within a short distance you will come to a stile and a waymarking arrow. Turn L over the stile and walk downhill, keeping the fence line to your L, and in 200 yards (180 m) you will arrive at a second stile (you will now be close to The Vision Farm, which is in private land to your L). Bear half R at this stile, following a waymarking arrow across a field down to the road. Cross a third stile, turning L onto the narrow public road, and go on for 1½ miles (2.5 km).

This little lane is a sheer delight and is reminiscent of what country roads were like before widening and improvement for modern traffic. Go past the small byre, through a gate, then on between variegated hedgerows to pass Garn Farm, a traditional old-fashioned farmhouse complete with tile-stone roof. The Afon Honddu follows the valley bottom to your R and several public paths cross over the river. Ignore all temptation to follow these diversions and continue on along the road. You will come to a sharp R bend just before Tafolog Bridge. Go straight on through the wooden gate, following the trackway through woodland and field for ½ mile (800 m) to reach a further tarmac road at Llwyn-on. The path is boggy in places because of pony-trekking, making bank-hopping necessary at the very muddy stretches. Follow the tarmac to a junction, turn L, go past the pub, then L again at a stile beside a large stone barn *(3)*. Walk across the field and back to the car-park beside Llanthony Priory *(4)*.

*1  Offa's Dyke Path*
This long-distance path follows, wherever possible, the ancient boundary established in the eighth century by Offa, King of Mercia. Offa's Dyke runs the length of Wales and was the cultural and military divide between the Celts to the west and the Saxons of the West Midlands. The massive earthen dyke, the first official demarcation line between England and Wales, was possibly created to symbolize Offa's power and prestige. There is no dyke on top of the Black Mountains, these forbidding uplands being enough of a barrier in themselves. Along other parts of the border —lower down toward the Bristol Channel, for example—good lengths of the original earth wall and ditch survive surprisingly intact.

Today, the dyke path serves as a pleasurable, if demanding, long-distance walking route for ramblers, stretching for 170 miles (272 km) from Prestatyn in the north to the Severn Estuary near Chepstow in the south.

*2  The Vision Farm*
The author Bruce Chatwin lived at The Vision Farm while researching material for his famous book *On the Black Hill*, now made into a successful film. It is a compelling, meticulously researched history of people and life on the Welsh borders from 1899 up to present times. The farm is not open to the public and walkers are requested not to knock on the door and ask to look around.

*3  Ancient building*
This is the original thirteenth-century gatehouse to Llanthony Priory. The great archway, tall enough to admit a loaded wagon, has been walled up and the building is now used as as barn. The apertures and detailing up above the arch add interest and character.

*4  Llanthony Priory*
St David built his cell here in the sixth century, and his

companion the hermit Issui lived nearby up on the hillside, beside the holy well of Patricio. Other solitary monks also lived in the valley during this 'Age of Saints', the golden age of the independent Celtic Church, enjoying the patronage and favour of Brychan, the Irish King of Brecknock (Brecon).

The priory was built much later, between 1175 and 1230, during the reign of Henry II, for the order of Augustinian canons. The building style is Norman and therefore very enduring against the ravages of strife, weather and time. The canons were not hermits, but a teaching order of religious gentlemen with extensive farms and properties in the valley and elsewhere. Constantly plagued by invading mountain bandits, the canons were not above defending themselves, and would set about the invaders with staves and swords. A most unorthodox feature of Llanthony is the unique little hotel—noted for its good beer—built into the fabric of this ancient religious site. A full guide to the priory is available, together with secular sustenance, in the hotel bar.

*The Vale of Ewyas is a secluded valley, locked away in the upper reaches of the Black Mountains.*

# BRECON BEACONS LINEAR RIDGE WALK

STARTING POINT
Small parking space at Blaen
taf-fechan (035173) or Forestry
Commission car-park a little farther
south (037170)
Both locations on Outdoor Leisure
Sheet 11
FINISHING POINT
Pont ar Daf car-park on the A470
(Outdoor Leisure Sheet
11/988198)
LENGTH
6½ miles (10 km)
ASCENT
1500 ft (460 m)

This demanding walk along the central mountain spine of the Brecon Beacons takes in the best-known features of the area, and offers panoramic views of the rugged mountain landscape along all of the route. Starting from the great green and golden bowl known as the Neuadd, the walk climbs up the straight road (probably Roman in origin) to the historic gap in the hills between Cribyn and Fan y Big. It then turns westward, going steeply up to Cribyn, and on along the high escarpment ridge towards Pen y Fan and Corn Du beyond.

This route is very exposed in bad weather to high winds, rain and poor visibility. A compass, map and adequate clothing are essential. Also, remember that the Beacons are infamous for fatalities as well as famous for their magnificent upland landscapes.

## ROUTE DESCRIPTION (Maps 16, 17)

From the parking space (or the spacious Forestry Commission car-park a little way south) turn L up the road. Turn R off the tarmac road onto a rough boulder-strewn trackway, leading along the edge of the conifers. This is the celebrated 'gap' road, thought to be a Roman track leading north across the hills toward Brecon and the ancient Roman fortress of Y Gaer just west of the town. Go on, climbing gradually uphill above the enclosed pasture land. After ½ mile (800 m) you will reach a steep gorge. This is the course of the Nant y Gloesydd, which cuts deeply across the track. The best way of crossing is to go down the easier L-hand path, jumping over the stream by the flat rocks below. Go on along the road walking steadily up into the Neuadd *(1)*, a huge amphitheatre in the centre of the hills.

The gap road skirts along the slopes of Tor Glas, passing above the Upper and Lower Neuadd Reservoirs, and climbs the long gradual slope up to the dip in the escarpment visible ahead. Pen y Fan and Corn Du are the main summits to your L, easily

*Opposite: On the summit of Pen y Fan, the highest point in South Wales*

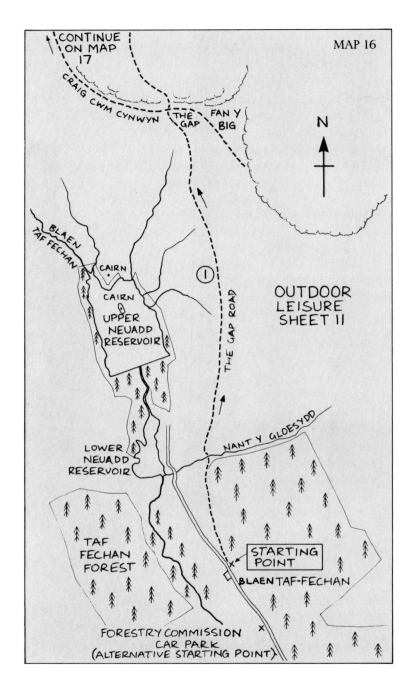

identified by their characteristic flat tops.

The gap itself is a distinctive worn gully at the highest point of the road and the stunning view northward into Cwm Cynwyn is a great reward for the long but gradual 2-mile (3 km) haul. This is a good place for a tea break and a look around at the hills. The sheer face of Cribyn looms above you to the L and Fan y Big is the summit with a long northward spur on your R.

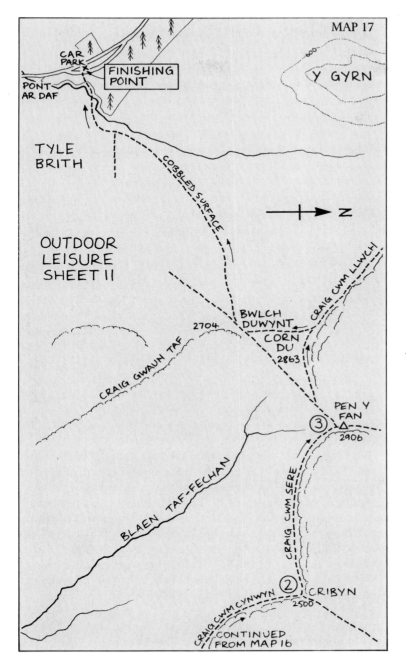

MAP 17

Y GYRN

CAR PARK

FINISHING POINT

PONT AR DAF

TYLE BRITH

COBBLED SURFACE

N

OUTDOOR LEISURE SHEET II

2704

BWLCH DUWYNT

CRAIG CWM LLWCH

CRAIG GWAUN TAF

CORN DU 2863

PEN Y FAN △ 2906

③

CRAIG CWM SERE

BLAEN TAF-FECHAN

② CRIBYN

CRAIG CWM CYNWYN 2500

CONTINUED FROM MAP 16

*Craig Cwm Llwch and its glacial lake from Corn Du*

The gap road goes on and downward from here, hugging the L side of the *cwm*. Brecon town can be glimpsed on the horizon.

From the gap go west straight up the steep path toward Cribyn, walking the long ridge of Craig Cwm Cynwyn for 1 mile (1.6 km) to reach Cribyn's summit. This part of the walk is deceptive, because when you think you have reached the top there always seems to be another long slope ahead. The view west *(2)* from Cribyn is one of the main features of the walk and takes in the central massif of the Beacon range.

The route ahead to Pen y Fan is laid out before you along the escarpment track of Craig Cwm Sere, leading first downhill then up again for 1 mile (1.6 km) to reach the final, very steep slope up to the obelisk and flat-topped summit. The last 200 yards (180 m) can be a little treacherous, particularly during wet weather, when the stones and muddy slope are very slippery. The view *(3)* from Pen y Fan never fails to impress, despite the over-popularity—and consequent serious erosion—of the summit and its approaches. On a Bank Holiday it can be difficult to find standing room here, at 2906 ft (886 m) the highest point in South Wales. It is always very windy on this exposed spot, and not very comfortable for any length of time.

Go on west from Pen y Fan across the saddle to neighbouring Corn Du. Then turn L, walking south-west along Bwlch Duwynt by the very worn path, to descend the steep slope of Tyle Brith for 1½ miles (2.5 km) toward the conifer plantation and car-park at Pont ar Daf on the A470 below. The eroded path cannot be missed, and lower down the National Trust is cobbling the surface in an attempt to stop the wear and tear.

Cross over the stream at the ford, walk through the gate at the forest corner and go on 500 yards (450 m) to your finishing-point at Pont ar Daf car-park.

*1 The Neuadd*
'The hall' is the literal translation of *neuadd*. Whether this refers to an ancient building that once stood here or merely to the steep walls of the surrounding hills is unclear. There was certainly an early settlement in the valley bottom and remains of this can be seen today. The small island in the upper reservoir has a Bronze Age cairn on top. The island itself may well be man-made, perhaps an ancient crannog (a raised area of dry land) built as a refuge in the middle of a swampy area.

The lake was created at the turn of the century, the great age of reservoir building, to catch the fresh springs and streams of the hills to provide drinking water for the industrial valleys of the south. The building style is Victorian Gothic, and this can be seen to good effect in the romantic tower jutting up above the surrounding pines. The tower is the outlet for the reservoir, where water pours down into a culvert below.

*2 View from Cribyn*
This view west from Cribyn is the showpiece landscape of the Beacons. The full height of the northern rampart of Pen y Fan is revealed—a drop of almost 1000 ft (300 m) from the summit to the slopes of Cwm Sere below. When there is snow on the ground is the best time of year to see this view, for then the strata lines of the great old red sandstone cliff-face are picked

out in dramatic black and white. Corn Du, the second summit, is a little to the left, behind Pen y Fan.

*3 View from Pen y Fan*

Looking north from Pen y Fan across the Usk valley there are fine views into the heartland of Wales, with the Cambrian uplands clearly visible on the horizon. The view westward looks past Corn Du across the wastes of Fforest Fawr to the Black Mountain and Fan Hir escarpment, while to the south the high ridge of Craig Gwaun Taf snakes its way along the west side of the Neuadd, down to the Taf Fechan Valley. The Pontsticill Reservoir chain can be seen among the conifers of Taf Fechan Forest beyond. Closer to hand is the line of the gap road, going down past the Neuadd Reservoirs to the walk's starting-point at the forest edge.

The little lake, high up on the northern slope just beyond Corn Du, is Llyn Cwm Llwch, the glacial lake of the deep *cwm* that stretches north towards the town of Brecon.

*Above the clouds on the summit of Corn Du*

# 3.15

# FOOTHILLS OF THE BLACK MOUNTAIN

STARTING AND FINISHING
POINT
Llanddeusant Youth Hostel car-park
(Outdoor Leisure Sheet
12/776245)
LENGTH
10½ miles (17 km)
ASCENT
600 ft (190 m)

This is a fairly demanding walk into the wilderness area of the remote Black Mountain. The walk starts from the Youth Hostel at Llanddeusant, following old farm lanes to reach the open hill above. It then changes to mountain track, to find and follow the River Usk, which flows down to Pont 'ar Wysg and the Glasfynydd Forest. The return journey across the beautiful hills of Fedw Fawr passes Arhosfa'r Roman Camp and descends into the intricate old footpaths of the Afon Llechach Valley. You will be exposed to the full force of wind and rain during bad weather and a compass is essential for navigation on the open mountain.

## ROUTE DESCRIPTION (Maps 18–20)

From the Youth Hostel car-park walk past the village's fourteenth-century church to the junction. Follow the road signposted Llyn y Fan for 250 yards (225 m) to a stile and farm track on the L. Walk up this old lane for ¼ mile (400 m), turn R at the waymarker post and continue uphill to reach the mountain gate at Pen Tyle. The rough mountain track ahead is one of the old Coffin Routes *(1)* and leads right over the mountain to the industrial valleys of South Wales. Climb up the steep hill ahead, following the rutted path due east above the magnificent Afon Sawdde Valley *(2)* for 1½ miles (2.5 km), crossing several stream courses to reach a gap in the hills below Bryn Mawr. The path divides here, near the valley bottom. Take the L fork and continue on a bearing of 60° magnetic for ½ mile (800 m) to find the glacial cutting of the River Usk flowing down from Fan Foel above. This appears as a broad, shallow valley with the river following a zig-zag course across the flat, stony floor. Look for a narrow sheep-path on the high L-hand bank and follow the Usk Valley for 1½ miles (2.5 km) on a bearing of 20°, to reach the bridge and tarmac road at Pont 'ar Wysg beside Glasfynydd Forest.

Cross the road, continuing along the L bank of the river to

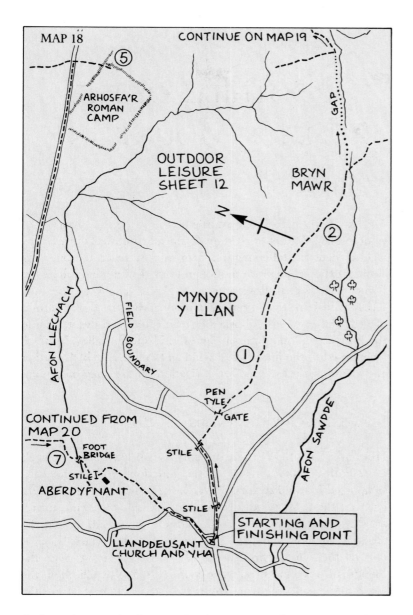

find a stile into the forestry land. Go across the water-meadow, following the river, to reach a hard forest track and ford. Do not cross the ford but go on over the meadowland to climb the high bank on the far side. The river enters the Usk Reservoir by a deep-cut channel below. For a sight of the reservoir and channel continue along the line of trees for 500 yards (450 m). Return by the same route. On returning to the forest road turn R.

Follow the forest road around the reservoir for 1 mile (1.6 km) to reach the far western end, where the open moorland of Fedw Fawr stretches south-west for ½ mile (800 m) to the deep gorge *(3)* of the Afon Clydach. Climb over the stile onto

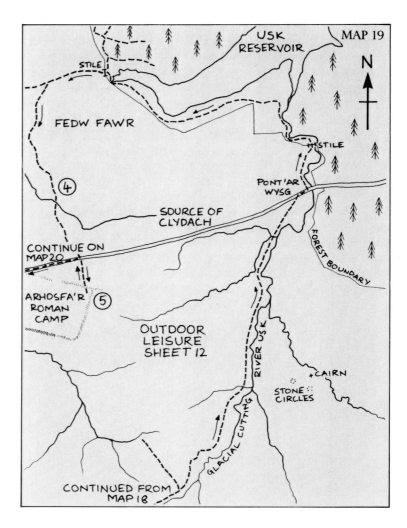

the moorland and walk along the valley bottom on a bearing of
250° magnetic, avoiding the lower marshy ground to find a well-
defined path above the gorge. Turn L and go south along the
rough moorland track for 1 mile (1.6 km) to reach the tarmac
mountain road. This is the best part of the walk for mountain
scenery, with the whole length of the Carmarthen Fans *(4)*
visible ahead.

The faint outline of Arhosfa'r Roman marching camp *(5)* can
be found on the hill above the road. Walk straight uphill,
looking for a line of very low earthworks at the sharp north-east
corner of the camp. Return by the same route. Follow the
tarmac road westward (i.e., to the L after returning), cross the
cattle grid and walk on for 1 mile (1.6 km) to the attractive Blue
Chapel *(6)* at Talsarn. Just beyond the chapel on the same side
of the road is a gate and entrance to an old public road. Walk
down this narrow sunken path into the valley, keeping R at the

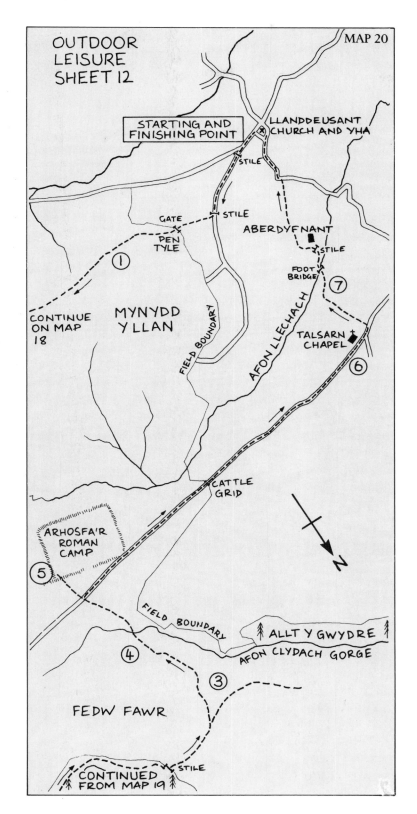

OUTDOOR
LEISURE
SHEET 12

MAP 20

STARTING AND
FINISHING POINT

LLANDDEUSANT
CHURCH AND YHA

STILE

GATE
STILE

PEN
TYLE

ABERDYFNANT

STILE

① FOOT
BRIDGE

⑦

MYNYDD
Y LLAN

CONTINUE
ON MAP
18

TALSARN
CHAPEL

⑥

FIELD BOUNDARY

AFON LLECHACH

CATTLE
GRID

N

ARHOSFA'R
ROMAN
CAMP

⑤

FIELD BOUNDARY

ALLT Y GWYDRE

AFON CLYDACH GORGE

④

③

FEDW FAWR

STILE

CONTINUED
FROM MAP 19

Overleaf: *The bulky, bare Black
Mountain from Mynydd y Llan*

first junction, to reach a field and track just beyond a makeshift gate. Turn R, follow the overgrown lane downhill to a stile and a bridge over the beautiful wooded gorge of the Afon Llechach *(7)*. Cross the river, walk on to the working farm of Aberdyfnant, bearing L at the farmhouse, to follow the hard lane steeply up, then carry on for ½ mile (800 km) to the tarmac minor road. Turn L and continue for a further ½ mile (800 m) along the road to the Llanddeusant Church and Youth Hostel.

*1 Coffin Routes*

The Industrial Revolution of the nineteenth century brought about a migration of labour from the rural areas to the new mines and quarries in South Wales. Dangerous working conditions caused many deaths among the workforce, which made necessary the regular conveyance of the dead back over the mountain for burial in Llanddeusant or Gwynfe. The rough tracks known as 'coffin routes' came into use, and the gambo-cart, a two wheeled vehicle pulled by a horse and the dead man's workmates, transported the coffin. There is a flat area at the half-way point, just below the summit of Fan Brycheiniog, where a short religious service was held before the coffin was handed over to mourning relatives.

*2 Afon Sawdde Valley*

This deep-cloven valley winds up into the hills to the source of the Afon Sawdde at Llyn y Fan Fach, a small glacial lake at the foot of Bannau Sir Gaer. The great cliffs of the old red sandstone escarpment dominate the skyline, towering above the lake and valley. This landscape is truly primeval and has changed little since rivers of ice shaped the hills and valley during the last Ice Age. The fields and small farms in the valley bottom date from the Middle Ages, and the field pattern remains largely unaltered since the Victorian period.

*3 Afon Clydach gorge*

Of all the streams and rivers that descend from the Black Mountain, the Afon Clydach is the most dramatic. The stream rises on the moorland of Fedw Fawr and plunges down into the deep, winding gorge, heading north-west through the wooded hills to join the Afon Bran near Myddfai.

*4 Carmarthen Fans*

Walking south above the Clydach Gorge reveals a whole panorama. In front looms the high wilderness of the Black Mountain, stretching up to the Carmarthen Fans. This mountain range is the western end of the great old red sandstone escarpment and marks the historical boundary of the ancient Kingdom of Brecknock founded by Brychan Brycheiniog, the eighth-century Irish king.

5 *Roman marching camp*

This square earthwork was made nearly 2000 years ago by a Roman legion while on the long march west to Carmarthenshire. The low walls, sunk to almost nothing over the centuries, were dug by the troopers in one evening before they settled down for the night. The camp would probably have been used by other marching columns and may have been a regular stopping point on this lonely stretch of Roman road.

6 *Talsarn Chapel*

The tiny Blue Capel (chapel) at Talsarn is one of many independent Methodist meeting houses built during the nineteenth-century revival of the movement. Methodism was quite a political force in its heyday, attracting a majority of the local population away from the Anglican Church. Many chapel members refused to pay the hated Church Tithe, levied on every family in the parish as the dues and living of the incumbent vicar. This popular dissent was later ratified in Parliament by the disestablishment of the Anglican Church in Wales and the subsequent abolition of the vicar's tithe. The present congregation at Talsarn is reduced to a handful of local farmers supporting the chapel out of their own resources.

7 *The old lanes*

These old agricultural lanes and paths are the remains of the nineteenth-century road system connecting farm dwellings. Parts of this Victorian infrastructure are still in regular use today for the passage of sheep and cattle.

*The empty moors near Pont'ar Wysg*

# Three Peaks

STARTING AND FINISHING
POINT
Parking area at Cwm Llwch camping
ground (Outdoor Leisure Sheet
11/006245)
LENGTH
9 miles (14 km)
ASCENT
2000 ft (610 m)

The famous peaks of the Brecon Beacons—Pen y Fan, Corn Du and Cribyn—dominate the mountain skyline and are the main objectives for most visitors to the National Park. The most popular route up to the summits from Storey Arms is known as the tourist route. This is best avoided by the serious walker on the grounds of both credibility and conservation, for the wear and tear on this track is already considerable.

A less-damaged and much more interesting linear walk to the tops starts from the woodland camping ground at Cwm Llwch. The first half of the walk is continually uphill, and although the ascent is gentle at first, it can come as a nasty shock to the inexperienced when the serious climb begins up the steep face of Craig Cwm Llwch.

Extra clothing is essential because conditions on the summits are nearly always more extreme than in the temperate lowlands. You should also bear in mind that there is no cover on the open mountain, so that the walker is exposed to the full force of wind and rain during bad weather.

## ROUTE DESCRIPTION (Maps 21, 22)

From the parking area go along the rough track, following the course of the Nant Cwm Llwch through tree-lined meadows. Cross over a wooden footbridge by a gate, then go on up the track to reach a sheep pen and a small building beyond. This was once a Youth Hostel but is now a private bothy rented by school and youth groups. Turn R at the waymark and skirt around the former hostel to reach two stiles, rejoining the track for a long climb up past low trees and bushes to a ladder-stile visible at the mountain boundary ahead.

The great vale of Cwm Llwch is laid out before you, with the twin peaks of Pen y Fan and Corn Du towering above; Cribyn, the third summit, is farther east, hidden behind Pen y Fan. The route ahead can be seen from the ladder-stile, leading diagonally up the R-hand side of the *cwm* toward the summit ridge above. Walk on past a pile of loose stone to find the established path,

*Pen y Fan's distinctive, flat-topped summit, seen from Corn Du*

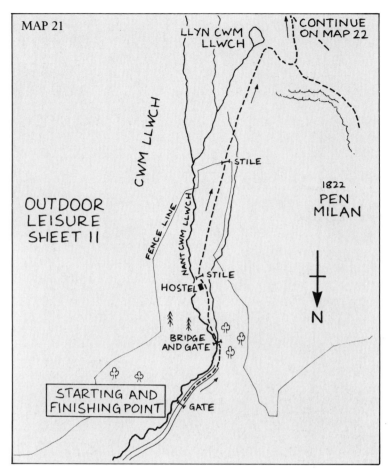

which goes steeply uphill for 1 mile (1.6 km).

The small glacial lake of Llyn Cwm Llwch will soon come into view down on your L. It is a good idea to stop at frequent intervals to catch your breath on this steep ascent, and to look around at the mountain landscape. The lake below is held back by a high moraine (earth wall) and was created by a glacier pushing up this wall of earth and stones during the final stages of the last Ice Age. The lake is the puddle of water left by the last of the melted ice.

Turn L at the top and follow the main track along the edge of the escarpment toward the summit of Corn Du ahead. Over to your R, and just hidden from view, is the famous Tommy Jones Obelisk *(1)*, a Victorian monument built in memory of a small boy who died on the Beacons. Go on by the very worn track up to the top of Corn Du, then on across the saddle to Pen Y Fan *(2)* for splendid views in all directions.

Descend from Pen y Fan on the far side, taking care when climbing down the steep and slippery path, to join the trackway

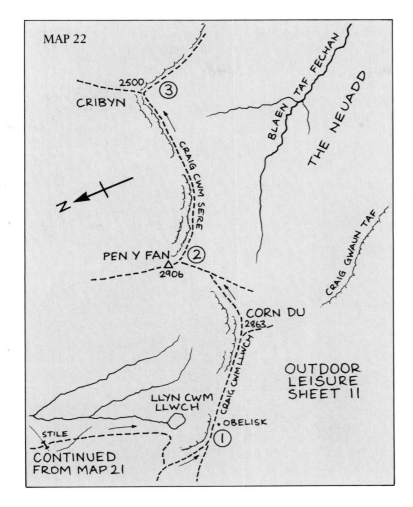

MAP 22

along Craig Cwm Sere, walking for 1 mile (1.6 km) along the top of the escarpment to Cribyn *(3)*, the summit directly east of Pen y Fan.

Return to Pen y Fan, then go back across the saddle to Corn Du. Follow the path of your outgoing route down the mountainside, passing the Tommy Jones Obelisk and Llyn Cwm Llwch, to reach the ladder-stile at the edge of the farmland. Go on down the track, cross the stiles at the former hostel and return through the meadowland to your starting-point.

*1 Tommy Jones Obelisk*

The obelisk in memory of Tommy Jones was erected by voluntary subscription to mark the spot where he died in 1900. On the night of 4 August, little Tommy, aged five, lost his way in the dark while walking between Cwmllwch Farm and the Login, straying up the steep mountainside toward the summit of the Beacons above. He finally collapsed and died of exposure here on the high ridge above Llyn Cwm Llwch. The people of Brecon searched the area around Cwmllwch Farm for twenty-nine days, not thinking that Tommy could have walked so far up the mountain. A Mr and Mrs Hamer of Castle Madoc near Brecon found Tommy's remains on 2 September, following a dream which Mrs Hamer had telling her of the exact place where his body lay.

2  *Pen y Fan*

This, the highest point of the Brecon Beacons, stands at 2906 ft (886 m), just 43 ft (13 m) taller than neighbouring Corn Du. Both summits have paid the price of popularity and are now seriously eroded by the boots of many thousands of walkers determined to get to the top. A number of suggestions have been put forward to relieve the problem, including making cobble-stone pathways a permanent feature of the mountain summits. The ground is now so damaged that any hard surface would seem an improvement on the present sorry state. However, many purist walkers would disagree, claiming this would limit their personal freedom of the hills and their right to wander.

As you look north across the Usk Valley there are fine views into the heartland of Wales, with the Cambrian uplands clearly visible on the horizon. The view westward looks across the wastes of Fforest Fawr to the Black Mountain and the Fan Hir escarpment. To the south, the long, high ridge of Craig Gwaun Taf snakes its way down to the Taf Fechan Valley beyond. The best view is eastward along the face of the old red sandstone escarpment. The distinctive strata lines of the harder brownstones stand out on the face of Cribyn, and continue along the cliff-face to Fan Big and the eastern headlands of Craig y Fan above the Talybont Valley. This landscape to the east reveals the true drama of the Beacons and is best viewed in the evening or early morning sun when the shadows and highlights are at their sharpest.

3  *Cribyn*

A delightful off-the-beaten-track summit, Cribyn is often by-passed by the long-distance walker, as there is a lower path on the southern side. The ancient 'gap' road from Cantref to Taf Fechan passes around the steep north-eastern slope of Cribyn, climbing up the west side of Cwm Cynwyn from the Usk Valley to the gap in the hills above the great amphitheatre of the Neuadd.

*The approach to Corn Du from Cwm Llwch*

# 3.17

# SOURCE OF THE USK AND LLYN Y FAN FAWR

STARTING AND FINISHING
POINT
Pont 'ar Wysg Forestry car-park at
the county boundary (Outdoor
Leisure Sheet 12/820272)
LENGTH
10 miles (16 km)
ASCENT
1050 ft (320 m)

This is a fairly demanding walk across large tracks of windswept moorland on the northern face of the Black Mountain. It climbs up to the foot of Fan Foel, then goes on around the mountain, to reach the isolated Llyn y Fan Fawr glacial lake below the steep face of Fan Brycheiniog. The first 6 miles (9.5 km) of the walk are continually uphill and map and compass work are essential for long trackless sections. This walk should not be attempted in poor visibility, as landmarks are an important aid to navigation.

Interesting features along the way include the glacial valley and source of the River Usk, the lakes and marshes of the mountain, Bronze Age sites and the Glasfynydd Forest.

## ROUTE DESCRIPTION (Maps 23–25)

Cross over the bridge, turn L at the Dyfed county-boundary sign and walk onto the moor along a worn track above the marshland. Follow this old sheep-path along the R side of the River Usk for ½ mile (800 m), crossing several small streams and areas of broken ground to reach the confluence of the Nant Tarw and the Usk just below a high embankment.

The river meanders across a plain of loose stones and boulders, constantly changing course and dividing into two or sometimes three separate watercourses. Standing pools of water, gravel banks and odd redundant loops can be seen, left behind by the eccentric passage of the Usk.

From the junction with the Tarw follow the Usk to the R, walking along the raised R bank above the river by a narrow sheep-path on a bearing of 200° magnetic. The tumbled landscape ahead is the shallow glacial valley *(1)* of the upper Usk. This valley deepens and narrows, with steep-sided walls of compacted soil and stones on either side, pushed up over half a million years ago by the enormous force of the moving ice. The river valley broadens again after 1 mile (1.6 m), bending around

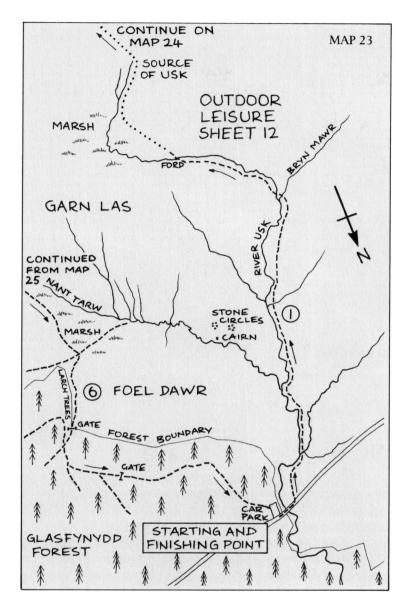

*Llyn y Fan Fawr*

to the L, then narrows suddenly into a gully heading south-eastwards towards Fan Foel. Walk around the R side, noting the zig-zag course of the river below.

Follow the Usk uphill on a bearing of 120° magnetic and continue for ½ mile (800 m), crossing over to the L bank when the ground proves too wet and boggy. You will come to a rough ford where several sheep-tracks converge. The loose stone of the ford is worth examining, as there are good examples of multi-coloured sandstones, including yellows, greens and pinks. From the ford walk on a bearing of 140° across the moorland to avoid an area of treacherous marsh visible ahead, rejoining the

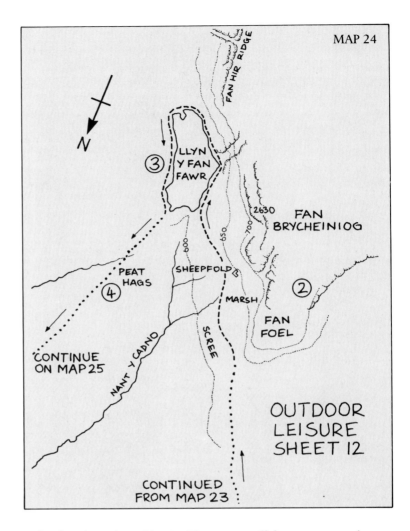

Usk after ¼ mile (400 m). The river will have narrowed to a mere stream and mysteriously disappears at intervals into a natural drain just below the surface. Follow the noise of running water, keeping R where two streams converge, to find the source of the Usk in a wet, swampy hollow with a large rock in the centre.

The Carmarthen Fans stand 1 mile (1.6 m) to the south. Walk uphill from the source of the Usk on a bearing of 160° magnetic to catch sight of Fan Foel *(2)*, the most westerly summit of the Black Mountain. Walk toward the base of Fan Foel, then on around the L side, following a narrow sheep-path across rocky ground above loose scree, close to the towering cliff. You will come to an area of wide marshland close to the foot of the mountain, contained by a hummocky earth wall on the left. This marsh is the remains of a drained glacial lake and the steep-sided embankment is a glacial moraine. Continue

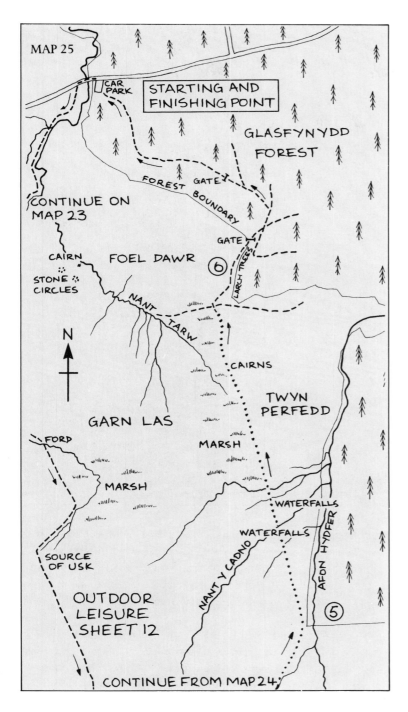

MAP 25

STARTING AND
FINISHING POINT

CAR
PARK

GLASFYNYDD
FOREST

FOREST GATE

FOREST BOUNDARY

CONTINUE ON
MAP 23

GATE

CAIRN

FOEL DAWR ⑥

STONE
CIRCLES

LARCH TREES

NANT TARW

N

CAIRNS

TWYN
PERFEDD

GARN LAS

FORD

MARSH

MARSH

WATERFALLS

WATERFALLS

SOURCE
OF USK

NANT Y CADNO

AFON HYDFER

⑤

OUTDOOR
LEISURE
SHEET 12

CONTINUE FROM MAP 24

along this high ground to the L of the marsh on a bearing of
150° magnetic, passing an old stone sheep pen, then on for ¼
mile (400 m) to the ridge above Llyn y Fan Fawr lake *(3)*. Walk
down to the water's edge, skirting the stony shoreline to the R
for a complete circuit of the lake, returning to the northern end.

The return route crosses the trackless moorland of Rhyd-wen Fawr and Garn Las. Set off on a compass bearing of 20° magnetic, walking for 1 mile (1.6 km) to the sharp corner of the conifer forest ahead. You will pass several large peat hags *(4)* on the way. These weird shapes, made of solid black peat with a topping of grass, are good examples of natural erosion.

The stream course at the forest corner is the Afon Hydfer, descending the mountain along a deep gully to reach the river valley below. The conifer plantation here has been recently felled *(5)*, leaving a landscape of considerable devastation. From the boundary fence continue walking across the open mountain on a bearing of 340° magnetic for 1½ miles (2.5 m), crossing two rocky stream courses with several attractive waterfalls. You will come to a wide marshland below Garn Las. This is the source of the Nant Tarw, an area of treacherous ground wired off in places to prevent sheep sinking without trace. Walk around the R-hand side of the marsh past several piles of loose stones. These are Bronze Age cairns, indicating that this area was once occupied by a community of primitive farmers who cultivated small fields and grazed stock on the mountain slopes. These early people lived on the Black Mountain 4000 years ago during the warm post-glacial period.

Just beyond the marshland is Foel Darw—the hill of the Nant Tarw stream—a distinctive dome-shaped landmark. Several established sheep-paths converge in the shallow valley below Foel Darw. Walk down to this junction and follow the clearly defined track at the base of the hill on the R, walking uphill toward the line of larch trees ahead. Then follow the very worn and eroded path *(6)* beside the forest boundary to reach a gate at a sharp corner of the fence. Beware of the very deep mud in front of the gate. Walk up the hard road into the trees, keeping L at the first three junctions, then on for 1 mile (1.6 km) by forest roadway through spruce and larch plantations to reach the car-park and your starting-point at Pont 'ar Wysg.

*1  Glacial valley*

During the last glacial period an enormous ice and snow cap formed on the summits of the Black Mountain. This ice cover extended into moving glaciers, spreading out across the landscape along the river courses, shaping and cutting the land with great force and forming many of the major geographical features that we see today. The Usk glacier, fed by numerous smaller tributaries, formed a principal valley feature along the whole length of the National Park.

*Remote Llyn y Fan Fawr is shrouded in legend*

*2 Fan Foel*

With a height of 2560 ft (780 m), Fan Foel is not quite the tallest peak in the Black Mountain. Neighbouring Fan Brycheiniog, just behind Fan Foel, occupies the same stretch of escarpment but rises to 2630 ft (802 m). Even if not the highest point, Fan Foel is certainly the most prominent feature of the Black Mountain range, particularly when viewed from the north and east.

*3 Llyn y Fan Fawr*

The larger of the two glacial lakes in this area, Llyn y Fan Fawr was scooped out approximately half a million years ago by ice flows descending from the heights above. The lake is contained by a moraine of earth and stones thrust up by the retreating glacier during the final stages of the last Ice Age. In January when Llyn y Fan Fawr freezes over to a considerable depth and deep snow clads the steep-sided fans, it is easy to imagine the interminable arctic winter that once gripped the Black Mountain for so many centuries.

*4 Peat hags*

The Black Mountain is covered with a thin layer of blanket peat. This primitive acid soil offers poor nourishment to the tough moorland grasses and in places where the surface vegetation has lost its hold, black-sided peat hags have appeared. These strange sculptures are slowly disintegrating, eaten away by frost and rain to form sterile black patches on the hillside.

*5 Conifer plantation*

Created in the 1960s, the upper Glasfynydd plantations have now been harvested and the enclosed land, naturally re-seeded with young spruce from the parent trees, will be left to grow into mature forest to be felled again in about thirty years. This afforested land is likely to remain under conifer indefinitely, changing the landscape for perhaps several hundred years.

*6 Erosion*

Overstocking of the grazing land has led to quite severe erosion around sheep pens on the lower mountain slopes. The area of Foel Darw in particular has been quite badly damaged by the frequent passage of sheep along the old trackways and over the surrounding moorland. Happily, significant changes in farming policy will shortly reduce the numbers of sheep grazed on the Black Mountain, relieving pressure on the open moorland to some extent.

*Hardy Welsh hill sheep need to be especially tough to survive the rigours of the Black Mountain*

# 4.18

# BLACK MOUNTAIN RIDGE WALK

STARTING POINT
Verge dropping-off point at public
footpath sign, Pont Haffes, Glyntawe,
on the A4221 (Outdoor Leisure Sheet
12/846165). Verge parking on the
nearby Pont Haffes minor road
FINISHING POINT
Llanddeusant Youth Hostel car-park
(Outdoor Leisure Sheet 12/776245)
LENGTH
12 miles (19 km)
ASCENT
1975 ft (600 m)

This arduous, linear walk from Pont Haffes at Glyntawe, on the eastern side of the Black Mountain, climbs up the rocky gorge of the Afon Haffes to reach the long southern slopes and knife edge of Fan Hir ridge above. It then goes along the escarpment to the summits of Fan Brycheiniog, Fan Foel and Bannau Sir Gaer above the Llyn y Fan glacial lakes. The route descends from the hills at Llyn y Fan Fach to follow the Afon Sawdde valley down to the Youth Hostel at Llanddeusant.

The walk is high-level for the majority of the way and is exposed to the full force of high winds and rain during bad weather. The first mile (1.6 km) is dangerous after heavy rain, as the river will be in full flood. An alternative route can be found along the left slope, crossing back over the river higher up where the Afon Haffes is a mere stream. A compass, Outdoor Leisure Sheet 12 (Brecon Beacons Western Area) and equipment for a full day on the hills are essential.

## ROUTE DESCRIPTION (Maps 26–28)

From the main road go along the public path past Carreg Haffes farm, bearing L at the first junction to reach a small metal gate at the foot of the steep-sided Haffes Gorge. Note the old stone sheep pen on the left when passing the farm buildings. Cross the Haffes at the ford, turn R and walk up the gorge, following the L-hand bank of the river. Take care across the boulders and glacial debris when choosing your route ahead.

The Haffes Gorge, with its piles of tumbled old red sandstone, swept down over the centuries, is a good example of the rugged landscape on this south-eastern side of the Black Mountain. After ½ mile (800 m) the watercourse hugs the left bank, flowing down a long straight chute of coloured pavement-stone, with numerous small waterfalls and attractive ferny grottoes to be seen. Cross over the stream where the steep slope makes walking difficult and go along the R bank for ¼ mile (400 m), recrossing the Haffes just before the steep crumbling scree on the right. Go on up the flat pavement-slabs, crossing the stream again where rocky ground makes the going difficult, to reach an attractive rock pool with huge slabs of stone above, which are crowned with trees, and a cascading waterfall beyond. This is the head of Cwm Haffes and the gateway to the high moorland of the remote Black Mountain.

Turn R and go straight uphill on a compass bearing of due north for 1 mile (1.6 km), passing a ruined stone sheep pen, then on up the long slope toward the Fan Hir escarpment, a sharp summit visible on the horizon ahead. You will pass through an area of large, square sandstone blocks, seemingly dropped from the heavens. These stones were left here during the Ice Age, deposited by a moving ice sheet flowing down from high above. Go on along the top of Fan Hir, walking northward for 1½ miles (2.5 km).

The steep cliff-face of the escarpment comes as quite a surprise, revealing a dramatic perspective of sweeping strata and high rampart wall, towering above the Tawe Valley below. The view beyond looks eastward across Fforest Fawr, the ancient hunting ground of the Norman Lords of Brecon, and Cnewr Estate, the biggest working sheep farm in Wales.

The bare and windswept wasteland to the west is the last true wilderness of South Wales. Designated a Remote Area *(1)* of the National Park, this upland region, set aside for silence and solitude, is bounded on the north side by the famous Carmarthen Fans, a line of cliffs and flat-topped highlands visible on the horizon to the north-west. Walk on northward toward Fan Brycheiniog, the eastern summit and meeting-point of the Carmarthen Fans and Fan Hir ridge.

Llyn y Fan Fawr, the larger of the two glacial lakes can be seen down below to your R. Go on past Bwlch Giedd, the steep-sided gully just above the lake, and join a narrow, worn path leading uphill to the top of Fan Brycheiniog *(2)*. The summit is marked by a concrete pillar with a stone shelter alongside. This windbreak, built by youth volunteers, is a good place for lunch in blustery conditions. If the weather is fine, go on to the farther summit of Fan Foel for superb views *(3)* northward into mid-Wales.

The cliff-face of Bannau Sir Gaer leads westward from Fan Foel along the summit ridge of Black Mountain to the smaller glacial lake of Llyn y Fan Fach. Go on along this cliff-top for 2 miles (3 km), walking downhill where the escarpment dips to Bwlch Blaen Twrch, then climb sharply up to reach the summit and cairn of Bannau Sir Gaer. Should the weather or visibility deteriorate, there is a narrow zig-zag escape route down into

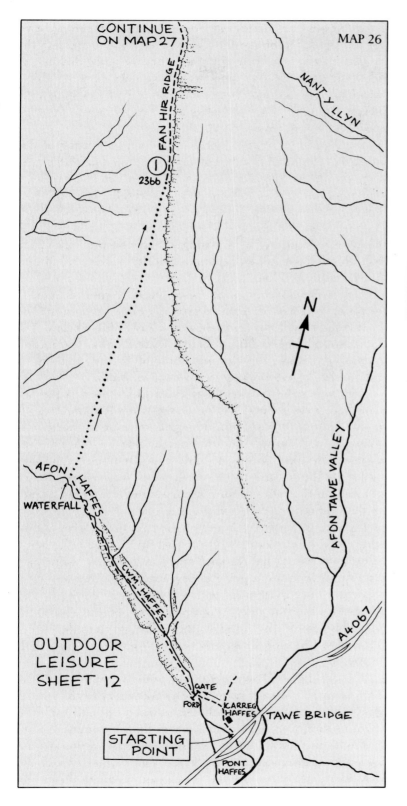

*Llyn y Fan Fach*

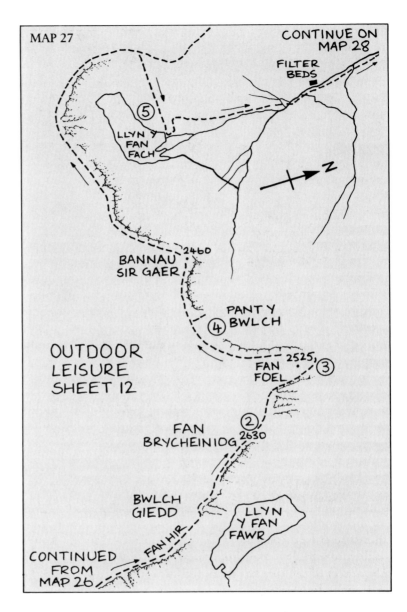

MAP 27

CONTINUE ON MAP 28

FILTER BEDS

⑤

LLYN Y FAN FACH

N

2460

BANNAU SIR GAER

PANT Y BWLCH

④

OUTDOOR LEISURE SHEET 12

2525

FAN FOEL

③

FAN BRYCHEINIOG

②

2630

BWLCH GIEDD

LLYN Y FAN FAWR

FAN HIR

CONTINUED FROM MAP 26

Pant y Bwlch *(4)* below. If you choose this short-cut, navigate from the foot of the cliff on a bearing of 290° magnetic for 1 mile (1.6 km) to reach the hard road.

The climb up to Bannau Sir Gaer is well worthwhile for a fine view southward. Swansea Bay can be seen as a gleaming circle of water and the Gower Peninsula is the long dark island-shape to the right. On a good day the North Devon coast is visible, with the hills of the Exmoor National Park to be seen on the far horizon across the wide Bristol Channel. Go on westward along the cliff-top for a sight of Llyn y Fan Fach, the magic lake *(5)* with an ancient legend of fairies and bewitchment. The

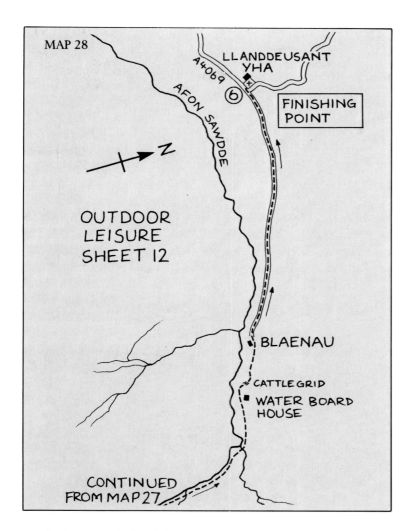

amphitheatre of the lake is a special place with a timeless quality, seemingly cut off from the worries of the outside world. The aspect of the lake has remained largely unchanged since the end of the last Ice Age.

Follow the worn sheep-path around the western slope, bearing R where the path descends, walking towards the small dam and little building at the water's edge below. The view of the escarpment is magnificent from here and provides a fine angle for a photograph of the lake and towering cliffs. The summit at the far end is Fan Foel, jutting out above the moorland like a huge natural pier.

Llyn y Fan Fach has been dammed at one end to increase the water volume for public supply. This work was carried out during World War I by conscientious objectors drafted in by the military authorities for heavy manual labour as the alternative to fighting in the trenches. The objectors con-

*Overleaf: The Black Mountain—like the central Beacons—has a severe, razor-ridged escarpment*

117

structed the dam, pipeline, filter station and road leading up to the lake.

Join the hard stone road and go on for 3 miles (5 km), down the beautiful Afon Sawdde Valley toward the tiny hamlet of Llanddeusant. You will pass the waterworks, keeper's house and Blaenau Farm to reach a junction. Go straight on, climbing gently uphill along the narrow, hedge-lined tarmac road through unspoilt farmland to the fourteenth-century Llanddeusant Church (6). There is a small pottery workshop in the old church stable opposite.

Look down into the valley for a fine view of the traditional field patterns and old woodland, dotted with an occasional farmhouse. The Carmarthen Fans at the head of the valley are displayed in all their glory and this is seen to best advantage some way along the road from just above Pencarreg Farm. The Old Red Lion Youth Hostel is behind the church. Alas, there is no beer to be found at this village pub, as the last pint was served in 1937 when the YHA bought the building, thus completing their chain of walkers' hostels through the uplands of Wales. The nearest pub nowadays is the Cross Inn, 1 mile (1.6 km) away.

*1 The Remote Area*

The National Park Authority purchased the Black Mountain in spring 1988, thus securing this wild upland region from inappropriate development such as coalmining or forestry. The Brecon Beacons National Park now owns all of the remote area to the west of Fan Hir and intends to preserve this unique landscape just as it is. There are no defined tracks across the wilderness and the single public path is very difficult to follow after the first few miles. This inaccessibility is one of the area's virtues and small groups of experienced walkers can enjoy the adventure of a truly wild landscape untouched by any human activity. The remote area has a number of rare plant species and the summits on the northern side are designated sites of Special Scientific Interest.

*2 Fan Brycheiniog*

Also called Bannau Brycheiniog, this highest point of the Black Mountain, measures 2630 ft (802 m). The border between the counties of Powys and Dyfed passes close to the summit and follows the approximate boundary of the old Kingdom of Brecknock. The summit itself is named after the Irish king, Brychan, who invaded South Wales and established Brecknock as his political power-base in AD 700, in the post-Roman period.

3 *Fan Foel*

Jutting out over the moorland below, Fan Foel commands panoramic views northward. The tumbled landscape in the foreground is the farming area of Llanddeusant, a hilly area of upland fields and deep, tree-filled gorges. The bare hills of Mynydd Myddfai stand directly to the north and the dark mass of Glasfynydd conifer forest surrounds the Usk Reservoir a little farther east. The upper Glasfynydd Forest has been recently felled, leaving a straight-edged block of devastation on the open mountainside.

4 *Pant y Bwlch*

The marshy land below is the site of a long-drained glacial lake, once similar to nearby Llyn y Fan Fach. However, the descending stream has broken through the surrounding moraine and now forms a chain of small marshlands along the course of the Afon Sychlwch.

5 *The magic lake*

Llyn y Fan Fach is the subject of an ancient legend, dating back to the twelfth century. The story concerns a magical lady clothed in white, who appeared from the water to bewitch a local shepherd boy. The young man, besotted by her beauty, requested the lady's hand in marriage. She agreed to his proposal and a bond was made with one condition: that he should not touch her with iron.

The couple lived happily at the nearby farm of Esgair Llaethdy for many years until the husband touched her by mistake with his stirrup iron. The marriage bond was broken and the lady promptly departed, returning to the dark waters of the magic lake and taking all of the farm animals with her. Historians suggest that this legend goes back to the arrival of the Iron Age people in Wales, and that the lady, with her fear of iron, may have belonged to the earlier Bronze Age population still living at that time in remote parts of the hills. The white lady continues to work her magic, for Llyn y Fan Fach attracts legend-seekers from many countries.

6 *Llanddeusant Church*

The church of the two saints, St Simon and St Jude dates from 1300 and was built on the site of a much earlier monastic community, founded by two sons of the Irish king, Brychan Brycheiniog. Brychan sent his many sons and daughters out to the far corners of the kingdom to spread the Christian Gospel, setting up chapels and small religious communities in remote places such as Llanddeusant. The present church, built with river stones gathered from the nearby Afon Sawdde, has been recently restored, giving a much-needed facelift to this venerable old building.

# THE PEMBROKESHIRE
# COAST NATIONAL PARK

*Broad Haven's huge beach*

*Opposite: FIGURE 3 The Pembrokeshire Coast National Park. The numbers indicate the approximate starting points of the walks.*

*St Govan's Chapel, hidden in the cliffs west of Broad Haven*

Each of Britain's ten National Parks is unique; every one has a distinct personality. Even so, many of them inevitably share common elements—landscape characteristics, for example. But the Pembrokeshire Coast National Park has an uncompromising uniqueness. Quite simply, there is no other National Park like it in Britain. Its inviolate individuality is summed up in its title: it is the only park to be coast-based. The boundaries of a few other parks encompass stretches of coastline, but such seashores are adjuncts to upland areas; they do not constitute the heart and soul of the park, as is the case in Pembrokeshire.

The park was formed in 1952, the fifth to be designated. It is the smallest of the parks, covering some 225 sq miles (58,250 hectares), with a long, narrow boundary that never ventures far from the coast (except along part of the northern shore where it curves inland for over 10 miles/16 km to embrace the Preseli Hills). It is also the only predominantly lowland National Park in Britain, a characteristic responsible for further distinctive features. For example, Pembrokeshire has twice the average population density of the other parks, and a much more intensive pattern of agriculture.

The name 'Pembrokeshire' has already been used by me very extensively. Consequently, any of the bureaucrats responsible for the creation, in 1974, of the new 'super-county' of Dyfed, and who happen to be reading this book, will be reminded yet again of their failure to erase Pembrokeshire from the map. The old county was swallowed up by Dyfed—a huge administrative area that extends from the tip of West Wales to the southern boundary of the Snowdonia National Park—but refused to be digested. The locals remain dogged in perpetuating the name Pembrokeshire. The newly created Preseli District Council in the north insisted on being known as the Preseli Pembrokeshire District Council. The southern part of the old county came under the South Pembrokeshire District Council. The embodiment of Pembrokeshire in the National Park's title must also have helped the cause. Today, Pembrokeshire's identity is as strong as ever. It may not exist officially. But try telling that to the locals.

Administratively, the Pembrokeshire Coast National Park Authority is guided, along similar lines to the Brecon Beacons, by a committee made up of appointees of the Secretary of State for Wales and representatives from various councils (county and district). The committee directs general policies and determines all planning applications—and notifications regarding agricultural development—within the park. It has three sub-committees, the responsibilities of which reflect the operational structure of the park's full-time staff.

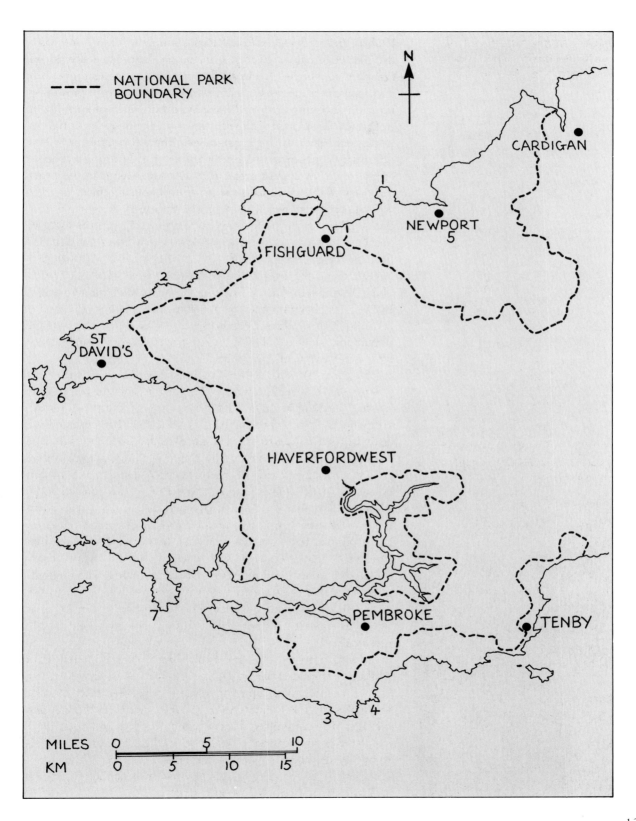

The areas of responsibility are:

(1) Forward Planning, which is concerned with research and long-term policy.

(2) Park Management, which deals with the construction, maintenance and management of fixed facilities such as the 186-mile (300 km) coast path, 500 miles (800 km) of other paths, car-parks, boat-parks, picnic sites and other facilities.

(3) Ranger and Information Services—responsible for general contact with the public, an extensive guided walks and talks programme, educational activities, park publications, and the operation of the park's Information Centres.

All of this may sound weighty, impenetrable and bureaucratic. Let me assure you that, for the walker in this part of Wales, the on-the-ground evidence of the National Park's work is accessible, lively and communicative. A free newspaper, *Coast to Coast,* is published each season, there are imaginative guided walks and special events, and the park operates a good network of helpful Information Centres which will point you in the right direction.

*Cliffs along the Dale Peninsula*

## SOME FACTS AND FIGURES ABOUT THE PEMBROKE-SHIRE COAST NATIONAL PARK

| | |
|---|---|
| DESIGNATED | 1952. It was the fifth of the ten National Parks in England and Wales. |
| AREA | 225 sq miles (58,250 hectares). |
| EMBLEM | The razorbill, chosen to represent the teeming sea-bird life for which the Pembrokeshire coast is internationally famous. |
| POPULATION | The 1981 census indicated that the total resident population stood at 21,531 (the park boundaries do not include the well-populated centres of Pembroke, Pembroke Dock and Milford Haven, but do include Tenby). The park's population structure—the ratio of males to females and the proportions in each age group—conforms very closely to the UK national average. |
| TOURISTS | An estimated one and a half million visitors came to the park in 1984, 90% of whom stayed in the area for an average of ten nights. With the recent trend of shorter, more frequent holidays and breaks, this 'long holidays' proportion may now be smaller, though the overall estimated fifteen million 'visitor days' a year is still valid. And this figure is increasing through improved accessibility along the M4 corridor. The pattern is highly seasonal, with about 150,000 visitors on a typical August day—as many as come in the six winter months combined. |
| WHERE TOURISTS STAY | A National Park survey of 1984 suggested that 60% of visitors stay in the park's south-eastern sector, in and around the main resorts of Tenby and Saundersfoot. The other 40% are fairly evenly distributed, mainly near the coast, with particular concentrations in the St David's and the St Bride's Bay areas. |

LAND OWNERSHIP IN 1987 (%)

| | |
|---|---|
| Private land | 85.7 |
| Ministry of Defence | 4.6 |
| National Trust | 4.2 |
| National Park Authority | 2.3 |
| Forestry Commission | 1.3 |
| Nature Conservancy Council | 0.5 |
| Other (e.g. local authorities and other public bodies) | 1.4 |

# THE FACE OF THE PEMBROKESHIRE COAST

## A PARK OF FOUR PARTS

Although the smallest British National Park, Pembrokeshire manages to pack into its confined boundaries a startling variety of scenery—everything from wild, open ocean coasts to the moorlands of the Preseli Hills, from small islands to vast beaches, from towering cliffs to wooded creeks.

In simple terms, the park has four parts. In the south, the park begins at Amroth, then runs through the popular resort area of Saundersfoot and Tenby, past sandy bays and spectacular limestone sea-cliffs, to the mouth of the Milford Haven waterway. The western sector, extending from this magnificent deepwater inlet to Solva, is dominated by the huge, crescent-shaped bite that St Bride's Bay takes from Pembrokeshire's west-facing coast. Farther north, the park boundary follows a rugged, serrated coastline, dipping inland to encompass the Preseli Hills, which rise to 1760 ft (536 m). For the park's fourth component, we return to the south: to the strange, unexplored Daugleddau, a wooded backwater in the upper reaches of the Milford Haven waterway.

## A SANCTUARY FOR SEA-BIRDS

The razorbill is the official symbol of the National Park, a reflection of the prime importance these coasts have as a habitat for huge quantities and myriad varieties of sea-birds. There is an interesting little story attached to the razorbill symbol. It was something of a compromise candidate, the more familiar profile of the puffin being the front-runner until it was pointed out that this particular bird has entered into a long-term contract with a certain publishing company.

Whatever the pros and cons of the razorbill versus the puffin, a sea-bird of some sorts it had to be. Even the least ornithological of observers will not fail to be impressed by the teeming colonies of birds that nest and breed here in almost every available cliff-face, sea-stack and offshore island.

Walkers are sure to catch sight of the razorbill somewhere along the route. This black and white bird, a member of the auk family, is to be found in huge numbers along the coast (and islands). There are a number of specific sites with exceptional bird concentrations. The spectacular sea pillars known as Stack Rocks (see Route 1.3, page 142), for example, just offshore from the southern coast, are home to the largest colonies of sea-birds that can be viewed from the footpath. They have the best-known auk colony in Britain, together with 1000 pairs of guillemots and about 130 pairs of razorbills—not to mention the fulmars and kittiwakes you can see here.

*Cwm-yr-eglwys's ruined church, Dinas Island*

This variety of birds can be seen along much of the coastline. Other birds that you are likely to spot include the cormorant and the oystercatcher. Cormorants, dark-coloured with a white face patch, are superb underwater swimmers and deadly in pursuit of fish. The oystercatcher is a familiar sight throughout the year as it pokes and probes the shore for food with its distinctive, long orange bill.

The most populous places of all are the offshore islands. Remote Grassholm, 12 miles (19 km) off the west coast, is perhaps the most impressive. This tiny rock is the home of over 30,000 pairs of gannets, making it one of the largest gannetries in the world. All in all, around 100,000 birds populate this lone rock. Skomer has one of the finest populations of sea-birds in north-west Europe. Fulmars breed here, as do shags, razorbills, puffins, guillemots, oystercatchers, kittiwakes and Manx shearwaters (around 100,000 pairs of the latter). This island, only a short distance off the Marloes Peninsula, is reached easily by boat during the tourist season. Skokholm, smaller and less accessible, has the honour of being Britain's first bird observatory, established in 1933 by the naturalist R. M. Lockley.

## CROMLECHS AND CELTIC SAINTS

Pembrokeshire is a paradise for those interested in prehistory. The area is littered with cromlechs (stone tombs), barrows, earthworks, stone circles, standing stones and encampments which reveal fascinating evidence of life in ancient Britain.

The best concentrations of sites occur in two areas: in the locality of St David's and in the Preseli Hills. Just west of St David's stands the important Neolithic site of Clegyr Boia, a tump at which remains of simple huts, stone axes and round-bottomed bowls (indicating an Irish connection) have been found. The settlement was fortified 2000 years later by Iron Age tribesfolk. On the rocky hillside above St David's Head around Carn Llidi there is plentiful evidence of Iron Age occupation. On the promontory itself stands Clawdd-y-Milwyr (the

Warrior's Dyke), an excellent example of a fortified cliff site. Its inner ramparts, with remains of drystone walling, together with outlines of circular huts, can still be seen. Beyond the fort there are fascinating traces of a field system, pointing to a mixed-farming pattern of cultivation, stock rearing and fishing. Nearby is Coetan Arthur, a cromlech with ubiquitous—and no doubt spurious—Arthurian connections. This is one of the scattering of tombs associated with the igneous outcrops between St David's Head and Fishguard, most of which are obscure ruins.

The most famous cromlech in Pembrokeshire—and possibly all of Wales—stands on the northern foothills of the Preseli Hills above Newport Bay. Pentre Ifan Cromlech is a stark collection of angular stones arranged as uprights supporting a massive 16 ft (5 m) capstone across the roof of the chamber. The tomb was constructed by Neolithic tribesmen around 3000–4000 BC for the communal burial of their dead. Carreg Coitan Arthur (yet another of the many traditional burial places of King Arthur), with its giant sloping capstone, is located nearby. The much-buried king is also said to rest at Bedd Arthur, a remote site above Crymych in the eastern Preselis.

The smooth, grassy skyline above Newport is interrupted by craggy outcrops. These are the remnants of a most impressive Iron Age hillfort built on the summit of boulder-strewn Carn Ingli (see Route 1.5, page 153). The Preselis also have stone circles, probably similar in purpose to the great circle at Stonehenge. Gors-fawr, for example, is a circle of sixteen stones a few miles south-west of Crymych. As with Stonehenge, the circle has been explained away as a gigantic sundial, with outlying stones placed in a deliberate alignment which has a special significance at the summer solstice.

The Preseli Hills have an even stronger connection with Stonehenge. In 1921 the geologist H. H. Thomas discovered that some of the monoliths in Stonehenge's inner circle were the Preseli 'bluestones', a spotted dolerite which is found at Carn Menyn and Carnbica in the hills west of Crymych. The effort required to transport these stones a distance of about 200 miles (320 km) must have been truly monumental. The journey was accomplished partly by rafts along rivers, and partly overland by hauling the stones on sledges under which rollers—probably logs—were placed. But no one has yet explained, in terms we can comprehend, the motivation which inspired this massive effort.

The peaceful, traffic-free highways and byways around remote St David's are today a million miles removed from all hustle and bustle. Yet in the fifth and sixth centuries, during the 'Age of Saints', St David's was, according to one historian, a

Opposite: *The spectacular curtain of limestone cliffs along the south Pembrokeshire coastline*

'veritable Piccadilly Circus'. In those times, sea travel was the safest, swiftest means of communication. The early Christian settlement of St David's became a busy crossroads, developing strong links with the Celtic countries of Ireland, Brittany and Cornwall.

David was born around AD 500. His austerity and frugality were soon recognized, for he became known as *Dewi Ddyfrwr*, David the Waterdrinker, in his missionary travels through Wales. The small monastic community that he founded, in a sheltered hollow hidden away from any approach by land or sea yet conveniently close to the coast, is now the site of the cathedral named after him. David's desire for a discreet location has been respected to this day. Visitors to his tiny city—a small enough place by any standards—are initially puzzled. Where is this grand cathedral that they have come to see? Eventually, its tall, square tower comes into view, well below the roof-tops, followed by the main body of the cathedral which almost fills a steep-sided, grassy bowl beneath the main street.

David's exceptional piety, and the vigour which he brought to spreading the Christian message, were officially recognized in medieval times. Canonized in 1120 by Pope Calixtus II, he is the only Celtic saint ever to be honoured in this way. The cathedral, a solid, purple-stoned building with magnificently carved roof timbers, was built between 1176 and 1198 after the coming of the Normans. St David is now more than a religious figure. As Wales's Patron Saint—St David's Day is 1 March—he helps express, along with the red dragon, the daffodil and the leek, the national identity.

## VIKING AND NORMAN INVADERS

*Sea rocks off Dale*

Pembrokeshire's map contains a scattering of strange, alien-sounding place names—Skokholm, Skomer, Gosker, Goultrop and Grassholm, for example—that sit uneasily with familiar Welsh and English names. They are Norse place names, a legacy of the Dark Age that befell these shores during the times of the Viking marauders. Between 982 and 989, for example, they sacked St David's four times, killing its bishop.

A hundred years later, the Norman invaders pushed west into Wales. The first to arrive was Roger de Montgomery, who built a crude castle of stakes and turf at Pembroke. This rough-and-ready stronghold must have been effective, for alone among the Norman castles in Dyfed it withstood the Welsh assaults of the following years. The castle was later rebuilt in stone. Visitors to Pembroke will appreciate why this later fortress was likewise never captured by the Welsh. The well-preserved castle, standing on a wooded crag above the river and roof-tops, still has an air of impregnability about it.

There are about fifty castles in Pembrokeshire. Most are obscure, overgrown ruins. Some—such as Pembroke, Carew and Manorbier—have stood the test of time and survive as stirring monuments to a troubled medieval period.

## THE LANDSKER

The pattern of distribution of Pembrokeshire's castles helps expain a strange phenomenon known as the Landsker, or 'land-scar'. This ghostly boundary—you will not find it on any maps—runs across country from Amroth to Newgale. Marked by a series of castles (now mostly ruined) at Amroth, Narberth, Llawhaden, Wiston and Roch, it effectively cuts Pembrokeshire in half. Although they had an influence north of this frontier, the Normans' strength was centred in the south. In their wake came Anglo-Saxon and Flemish immigrants: the 'little England beyond Wales' of South Pembrokeshire was born.

The map of Pembrokeshire reflects the cultural difference between the English-speaking, church-going south and the Welsh-speaking, chapel-worshipping communities of the north. 'Little England' is dotted with alien place names such as Rosemarket and Templeton, while traditional influences reassert themselves in the northern 'Welshry' at villages like Llandysilio and Maenclochog.

The Landsker had real significance for many centuries. Villages facing each other on either side of the line had little in common. Intermarriage was forbidden between couples living close together but separated by the Landsker. Today, the Landsker's influence has waned, though if you are of a romantic or mystical frame of mind, you might disagree. An alternative theory concerning this strange boundary states that the Landsker reflects man's immutable, deep-rooted relationship with the earth on which he stands. The line, so the theory goes, is a manifestation of the underlying geology, separating North Pembrokeshire's rugged, resilient rocks—among the oldest in the British Isles—from the softer, much younger rocks in the south.

## THE PEMBROKESHIRE COAST PATH

This marvellous path was seventeen years in the making. The

*Walkers must take heed of the warning flags at the Castlemartin Firing Range, which adjoins a memorable south Pembrokeshire cliff walk*

idea was first approved in 1953, and the path was officially opened on 16 May 1970, the third long-distance footpath in Britain and the first in Wales. But how long is long-distance? The official length of 186 miles (299 km) has been disputed by many pedantic souls. Estimates range from 180 to 200 miles (290–322 km), not that the overall length matters unless you are one of those walkers who likes to log, to the nearest decimal point, distances covered.

The path runs from St Dogmael's, near Cardigan, in the north to Amroth in the south. It is not quite a continuous coastal route owing to the interruptions caused by developments along the Milford Haven waterway and military activity along a short stretch of the south coast. For the most part though, the path stays as close to the cliff-edge or high-water mark as possible. Although there are some steep sections and lots of localized 'up and down' stretches between sea level and cliff-top, there are none of the endless uphill slogs you find in mountainous terrain. Many parts of the path are suitable for casual walkers. But a note of caution needs to be sounded here: at times, the path skirts very close to dangerous, unguarded drops, so children should be kept under control at all times and not allowed to wander away from the path or the adults.

In addition to the stunning views, another thing you will notice en route is the stiles. There are hundreds and hundreds of them, so many—about 500 in total—that I have only mentioned in my walks those that act as significant landmarks in the route descriptions and on the maps. Route-finding is easy. The route of the path is self-evident and/or well waymarked throughout most of its length. This is one area in which you should not get lost!

About 600 dedicated souls walk the entire length of the path each year. (Some macho walkers claim to have completed it in three and a half days; ten to fourteen days is a more reasonable—and much more enjoyable—timespan.) Most visitors to Pembrokeshire walk short stretches of the path. The following walks have been chosen as a representative cross-section, taking into account geographical distribution and different types of coastal scenery. One route, away from the coast path but still within the boundaries of the National Park, ventures into the uplands of the Preseli Hills.

*The Holy Well at St Non's Bay*

# SELECTED WALKS IN THE PEMBROKESHIRE COAST NATIONAL PARK

*Harbour markers guide vessels into Porthgain's narrow entrance on the rock-bound north Pembrokeshire coast*

# 1.1

# DINAS ISLAND

STARTING AND FINISHING
POINT
Car-park at Cwm-yr-eglwys
(Pathfinder Sheet SN 04-14/015401)
LENGTH
3¼ miles (5 km)

This wonderful little walk will take you right around Dinas Island (an island in name only: it was cut off from the mainland 8000 years ago but is now linked to it by a low-lying valley). Walkers are rewarded with expansive views eastwards and westwards along the Pembrokeshire coast, and a glimpse of teeming bird life. The walk is suitable for all the family, as long as extra-special care is taken with younger children on certain sections of the route where the path passes close to abrupt drops to the sea.

## ROUTE DESCRIPTION (Map 29)

From the car-park near the church *(1)* follow the metalled road up the hill. Within 150 yards (140 m) turn R at the footbridge, following the sign for the coast path, and climb up the side of the thickly wooded and bracken-covered hillside above Cwm-yr-eglwys. Within about 250 yards (225 m) go over a stile into open countryside, where you will enjoy magnificent coastal views eastwards to Cemaes Head and the start of the Pembrokeshire Coast National Park.

On the approach to Needle Rock *(2)*, the path narrows as the grassy hillside becomes steeper. Continue past the rock and climb up a series of steep steps to a stile. For the next ¼ mile (400 m) or so, the narrow path hugs the cliff-tops, often close to the edge—so great care should be taken.

Pwll-glas, a huge, black, sea-washed rock, comes into view and the hillside becomes a little less precipitous. (The latter is carpeted in a splendid display of bluebells in late spring.) Follow the path up the flank of the hill to Dinas Island's 463-ft (141 m) summit of Pen-y-Fan, which stands directly above Dinas Head. From the OS obelisk, there are more superb views, this time westwards along the coast right into Fishguard Bay, where the ferry boats from Ireland dock, and farther west again to St David's.

Follow the path downwards along the exposed, west-facing coast of Dinas Island, for ¾ mile (1.2 km). On the approach to

134

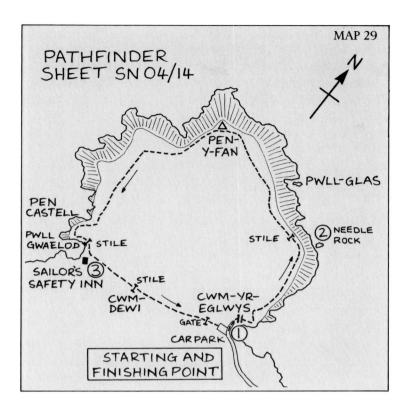

Pwll Gwaelod, the path descends abruptly, passing close to the cliff-edge above the shingle cove of Pen Castell before joining the metalled road above the pretty sandy beach at Pwll Gwaelod.

At the stile, turn half R and walk down this metalled road towards the Sailors' Safety Inn *(3)*. Just before the inn, turn L at the PFS and follow the path along the little valley of Cwm-Dewi (a glacial melt-water channel), past marshy ground to the R. Within ¼ mile (400 m) go straight on over a stile. On the approach to Cwm-yr-eglwys, go through the gate and follow the path along the side of a small caravan park next to the car-park, the starting-point of the walk.

*1 Cwm-yr-eglwys*
The Welsh name of this pretty little village means 'the valley of the church'. Unfortunately, the church, which overlooks the sea, is in poor shape. Only the belfry and part of the west wall remain of this twelfth-century Celtic-style church. It was wrecked by a huge storm in October 1859 which also claimed over 100 ships off the Welsh coast. A religious site may well have been founded here as early as the sixth century, for the church is dedicated to St Brynach, an early Christian missionary from Ireland.

2 *Needle Rock*
The path overlooking this angular sea stack is a perfect vantage point for bird-watchers. The rock, a thriving bird colony, is at its busiest between April and July. Herring gulls, razorbills, great black-backed gulls, shags, feral pigeons and guillemots nest on the rock, while fulmars, rock pipits and jackdaws nest on the cliffs just below the path.

3 *Sailors' Safety Inn*
This unusually named inn, which dates back to the late sixteenth century, has always displayed a light at night to help guide ships across Fishguard Bay. It is also one of the few pubs located on the coast path—so make the most of it.

*Pwll-glas (in the foreground) and Needle Rock, Dinas Island*

# TREVINE TO ABEREIDDY

STARTING POINT
Small parking area off coast road just
west of Trevine (Pathfinder Sheet
SM 83-93/834324)
FINISHING POINT
Car-park beside Abereiddy beach
(Pathfinder Sheet SM 62-72/798314)
LENGTH
3¾ miles (6 km)

On this walk, you will come across some of the strangest places along the Pembrokeshire coast. Abandoned industrial sites and quarries (one of which is submerged) appear unexpectedly along an otherwise unspoilt coastline; not that these abandoned sites altogether mar their settings, for in themselves they possess an unorthodox beauty.

## ROUTE DESCRIPTION (Map 30)

Park the car at the bottom of the hill. First visit Trevine's old corn mill (1) by following the path opposite the row of cottages down to the mill ruins, 50 yards (45 m) off the coast road. Then retrace your steps back onto the road and walk up the hill. At the farm on the R near the top of the hill, follow the signpost for the coast path and turn R, through the gate and past the farm. Within 200 yards (180 m), you leave the farm behind as you go through a gate onto a grassy headland above a line of cliffs.

For the next mile (1.6 km), the well-defined coast path crosses a number of stiles as it runs beside the boundary of cliff-top fields. At the stile near the approach to Ynys-fach, keep to the R of the field boundary. After the next stile (within about 250 yards/225 m) the path skirts the top of eroded cliffs, giving fine views of grass-topped Ynys-fach just offshore.

At the next stile (again within about 250 yards/225 m of the previous stile) turn half R and follow the path around Trwynelen headland, which commands panoramic views along the coast. As you approach Porthgain, two strange objects come into view—a pair of tall, inverted cones. These are the towers which mark the narrow, rock-bound entrance to Porthgain harbour (2).

The path descends via the eastern marker tower (or you can take a well-defined short-cut) to the quayside. At the western end of the quay turn back half L up a series of steep stone steps to the headland. Follow the path in the direction of red-bricked ruins across terrain which shows plentiful evidence of past industrial activity. On the approach to the ruins, the path runs

Overleaf: *Porthgain harbour*

beside the line of an old tramway (on the R) leading to a quarry.

Beyond the quarry, Pembrokeshire's natural beauty reasserts itself. From the path there is a fine view of the arch on the narrow-necked Penclegyr promontory above Porth Dwfn. Continue on the path above Porth Egr, then follow the line of the fence to a stile above the bay, where there is access to the attractive sandy beach of Traeth Llyfn. Follow the path west across steep cliffs and on the approach to Abereiddy *(3)* another navigation tower comes into view. Skirt the base of the Trwyncastell promontory, past the viewpoint for the 'Blue Lagoon', and follow the path down to the car-park by the black sands of Abereiddy beach.

*1 Melin Trevine Mill*

Although abandoned and quiet now, this mill was once a busy place. The cottages opposite were the homes of quarrymen and fishermen, and trading boats made their calls. For 500 years, the mill was vital to the life of Trevine. Wheat was milled here into flour for bread, and barley was ground to provide winter feed for cattle and pigs. But by the early twentieth century, the advent of cheap grain from overseas, larger, more efficient mills located in the towns, and improved communications between urban and country areas dealt a death blow to local village mills such as this. In 1918, the mill closed.

*2 Porthgain*

If it were possible to remove the remains left by the quarrying industry—the great stone shell of the crushing plant and the ruined hoppers along the quayside—Porthgain would look like the perfect smugglers' cove. The narrow entrance to this sheltered little harbour makes it the ideal hideaway on North Pembrokeshire's rock-bound coast. Yet in the nineteenth and early twentieth centuries, this quayside was a hive of activity as ships queued for their cargoes.

Porthgain's industrial past is based on slate and granite quarrying, brick making and the production of stone and chippings for the roads of Britain. Slate, granite and bricks were much in demand in Britain's rapidly growing nineteenth-century urban and industrial centres (many public buildings in London and Liverpool are of Porthgain granite). As this trade declined in the early twentieth century, another grew to replace it. With the advent of the motor car came the need for properly surfaced roads, for which Porthgain's crushed granite was ideal. The boom was big, but comparatively short-lived. By 1931, the trade was over.

This odd place has a beauty all of its own, and the various

*Trwyncastell headland*

remains tell a fascinating tale. Evidence of industrial activity is not confined just to Porthgain. The headland above the harbour is gouged by quarries, and the trackway of the 3-mile-long (5 km) railway that once connected Porthgain to Abereiddy can still be traced.

Be sure to call in at Porthgain's Sloop Inn, a typical harbourside pub dating from 1743, where there is a display of old photographs depicting the quayside in its heyday.

3 *Abereiddy*

Abereiddy's industrial prosperity was based exclusively on slate. Scant ruins, the remnants of workers' cottages, stand above the beach, which has an unusual dark sand produced by the erosion of the area's black, shaly rocks. A striking reminder of the slate industry can be seen on the eastern headland, where a deep quarry has been flooded by the sea to form a spectacular feature known as the 'Blue Lagoon'.

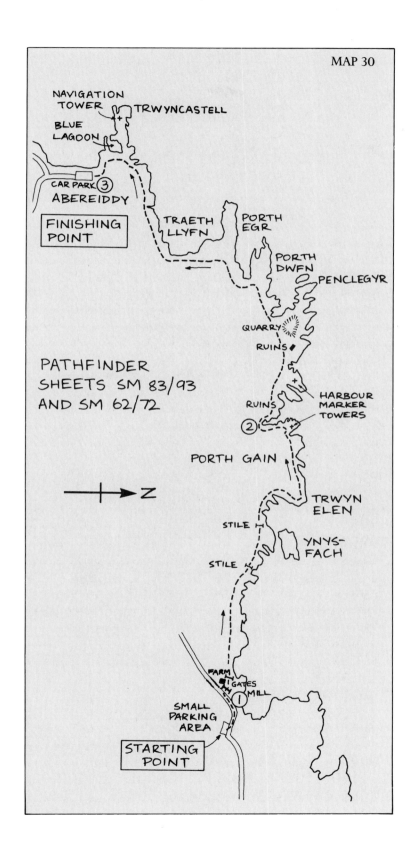

# STACK ROCKS TO BROAD HAVEN

STARTING POINT
Car-park at Stack Rocks on the Royal
Armoured Corps Castlemartin Firing
Range (Pathfinder Sheet
SR 89-99/925946)
FINISHING POINT
National Trust car-park above Broad
Haven beach (Pathfinder Sheet SR
89-99/976938)
LENGTH
5 miles (8 km)

This windy, exposed walk will take you across grassy headlands, flat for much of the way. There is nothing tame, though, about this route. Those headlands sit on top of southern Pembrokeshire's spectacular curtain of limestone cliffs, coastal scenery at its most awesome. Two of the most impressive sights can be seen right at the start of the walk—the famous sea-arch known as the Green Bridge of Wales and the neighbouring pinnacles of Stack Rocks.

Access to this walk is dependent on military activity—or rather the absence of it—on the Royal Armoured Corps Castlemartin Firing Range. When the range is in use, the road off the B4319 to the car-park at Stack Rocks is closed, as is the coast path from Stack Rocks to St Govan's Chapel (a distance of 3½ miles/5.5 km). When firing is taking place, there are warnings by red flags by day and lights by night, on flagpoles and control towers.

In strict terms, this 5-mile (8 km) walk appears out of order in the book. It comes before the 3-mile (5 km) Broad Haven to Stackpole Quay walk (see Route 1.4, page 148) since the two can be joined together to create a continuous 8-mile (13 km) walk. The split comes at Broad Haven for a very good reason: just above the beach are the Bosherston Lakes, freshwater ponds famous for their waterlilies and wildlife, which are accessible by a detour off the coast path. (The detour is described at the start of the next walk.)

## ROUTE DESCRIPTION (Maps 31, 32)

From the car-park, turn half R and walk across the cliff-top turf for 300 yards (275 m) to the viewing platform for the magnificent Green Bridge of Wales (1). From here walk east along the cliffs to Stack Rocks, also known as Elegug Stacks (2), where you pick up the coast path proper at the gate into the firing range (3). (The area immediately west of the Green Bridge

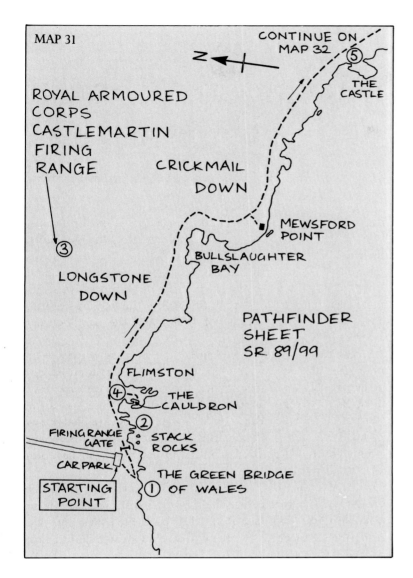

CONTINUE ON MAP 32

is closed to the public at all times.)

Take note of the warning signs. Children are warned not to touch anything lying on the ground which could be dangerous (shells or bullets, for example). Follow the line of white markers, which determine the path right the way through the range. Do not let this necessarily overt evidence of military activity put you off, for everything is eclipsed by stunning coastal scenery as cliffs plunge vertically into the sea in a great, jagged curtain of limestone.

From Stack Rocks, there is easy, airy walking on the flat path across well-cropped turf. To the L is the bleak, open expanse of Longstone Down and, in the distance the tall chimneys of Milford Haven's petrochemical plants.

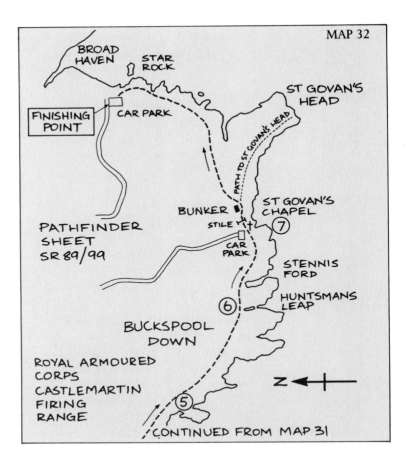

At the peninsula of Flimston, it is possible to take a detour R off the path beside the pronounced, well-preserved defences of an Iron Age fort *(4)* to the spectacular Cauldron at the end of the rugged little promontory. Continue eastwards along the wide, well-defined pathway, past Bullslaughter Bay, in the direction of the coastguard lookout station at Mewsford Point for a superb, though precipitous, cliff-edge view back along the coast.

Then rejoin the path (a short detour will have been necessary to reach the view-point) and walk along Crickmail Down and Buckspool Down past The Castle promontory, with its ingenious Iron Age fort *(5)* and evidence of modern military activities in the form of a radar station on its south-eastern approach.

After The Castle, continue on open grassland away from the cliffs and sea-views for ⅓ mile (800 m) to the spectacular chasm known as Huntsman's Leap *(6)* and, next to it, a second, wider ravine, called Stennis Ford. Within ¼ mile (400 m) turn R opposite the car-park and go down the steps cut into the cliff for St Govan's Chapel *(7)*.

Return to the cliff-top and follow the metalled path leading east from the car-park. Very soon, cross over a stile signposted coast path. Within 200 yards (180 m), bear half L—the turning is unsignposted and slightly hard to spot—off the metalled path at a low, bunker-like building. Go past the bunker on your L and across gorse-covered heathland, following the white markers. (If you stay on the metalled path, you end up at St Govan's Head.)

Continue along the path for another mile (1.6 km) to the car-park on the headland above Star Rock and Broad Haven beach.

*1  The Green Bridge of Wales*
This famous example of marine erosion has an arch around 80 ft (25 m) tall. The 'bridge' has been produced by a pounding sea which has joined two caves originally on opposite sides of an old headland.

*2  Stack Rocks*
The next stage on from the Green Bridge in the cycle of marine erosion can be seen at the neighbouring Stack Rocks. These massive limestone pillars were once connected to the mainland by arches which have now collapsed, leaving a pair of towers marooned offshore. The flat-topped Elegug Tower, 150 ft (45 m) high, is the tallest; the Elegug Spire, with its pointed summit, stands 130 ft (40 m) high. Both rocks are a mecca for birds and a magnet for bird-watchers. Stack Rocks' sea-bird colonies are the largest in Pembrokeshire that can be viewed from the path. The inhabitants include guillemots, kittiwakes, auks, fulmars and razorbills. The rocks are at their most densely populated in the nesting times of spring and early summer.

*3  Royal Armoured Corps Castlemartin Firing Range*
This large tank gunnery range of 5884 acres (2380 hectares) is one of Western Europe's most important NATO training areas. It extends down to the finest stretch of limestone-cliff coastline in Pembrokeshire, preventing public access to the coast path when military exercises, including tank and weapon training, are taking place (the coastline west of the Green Bridge up to Freshwater Bay is permanently closed). From the path, you can see the detritus of military activity—mangled tanks, bunkers and targets—scattered across the flat, rough grasslands.

*4  Flimston Iron Age Fort*
This rugged promontory is defended by a series of banks with a well-defined entrance at the centre and traces of hut circles. Just below the fort is the Cauldron, an aptly named blowhole 150 ft (45 m) deep. Take special care on the rocks here.

*Near St Gordon's Head*

5 *Buckspool Down Iron Age Fort*

This encampment makes even better use of natural features as an aid to defence. The cliff-bound promontory is protected not only by the usual earthen barrier; a blowhole has been cleverly incorporated into the defences. (Blowholes, through which the sea gushes and spouts during gales, are a feature of this stretch of coastline.)

6 *Huntsman's Leap*

The legend surrounding this deep, narrow sea-fissure is almost believable. A horseman, after jumping this chasm, looked back and died of shock! This fault in the rocks is indeed a remarkable natural phenomenon. Its sheer cliffs—a popular rock-climbing venue—drop away to a gloomy, sea-filled ravine 130 ft (40 m) below.

7 *St Govan's Chapel*

A steep flight of worn steps, cut into the limestone, leads down to this tiny chapel built into the base of the cliffs just above the sea. Originally a hermit's cell of the sixth century, the chapel as it now stands dates largely from the thirteenth century. It is probably dedicated to an Irish abbot and contemporary of St David known as Gobhan, who died here in AD 586. St Govan's holy well was said to have miraculous healing powers, with the ability to cure eye troubles and crippled limbs. It was a place of pilgrimage until the mid-nineteeth century, but is now dry.

# BROAD HAVEN TO STACKPOLE QUAY

STARTING POINT
National Trust car-park above Broad
Haven beach (Pathfinder Sheet
SR 89-99/976938)
FINISHING POINT
National Trust car-park at Stackpole
Quay (Pathfinder Sheet
SR 89-99/992958)
LENGTH
3 miles (5 km)

This walk combines spectacle and scenic variety. Stackpole Head is undoubtedly the most impressive feature along the route. The walk also takes in two exceptionally attractive, sandy beaches—Broad Haven and Barafundle—and, on a slight detour, the unusual freshwater lily ponds at Bosherston. The route is easy, but there is the usual proviso concerning the steep Pembrokeshire cliff-top paths and sudden drops to the sea. By combining this walk with the preceding Route 1.3, you can create a continuous route of 8 miles/13 km (see the note in the introduction to Route 1.3 on page 142).

## ROUTE DESCRIPTION (Maps 33, 34)

From the National Trust building at the car-park, pass Stackpole National Nature Reserve information board and follow the path down to Broad Haven beach. Walk along the edge of this attractive, sheltered beach, following the line of the sand dunes. At the northern end of the dunes, bear L along the narrowing stretch of sand leading to the neck of the beach. Then continue along the remainder of the beach, crossing a few boulders on the approach to the narrow strip of land, a barrier between salt-and freshwater, that separates the beach from Bosherston Lakes *(1)*.

At the lakeside signpost here, bear R toward Stackpole Head. (This signpost is also the point of departure from the coast path for those wishing to take a circular walk around the banks of Bosherston Lakes.) Continue on the path and within 100 yards (90 m) ascend a log staircase laid across the fragile dunes, climbing to a grassy headland with good views of the lakes.

Follow the path to Saddle Point, where the angular, towering sea-cliffs of Stackpole Head come into view. Go past a spectacular blowhole on the R (one of the many along South Pembrokeshire's limestone coast), its sea-filled basin sunk deep into the headland. Continue on for ¼ mile (400 m) to the stile

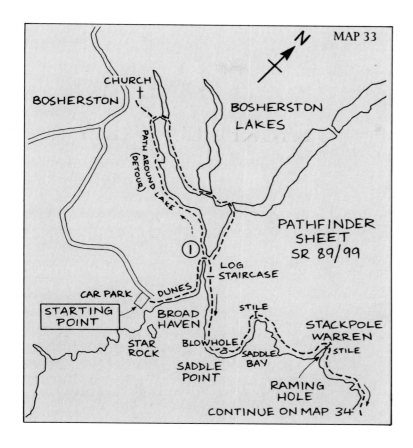

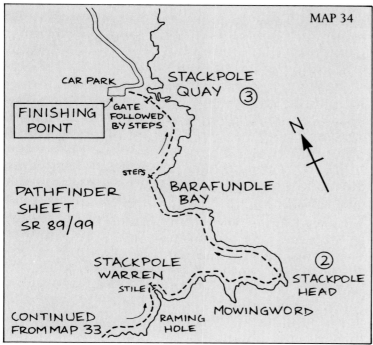

above Saddle Bay, a small, sandy, cliff-bound bay with very steep, difficult access.

From the stile, follow the yellow waymarked posts across Stackpole Warren headland (the grassland here is peppered with rabbit holes). These posts come to an end at the stile beside the narrow sea-fissure known as Raming Hole. Turn R here along the path beside the cliffs for Stackpole Head. The path first passes the lesser promontory known as Mowingword before running around the wild, windy and truly spectacular Stackpole Head (2). Take special care on this exposed, precipitous headland, particularly on a gusty day.

Continue on the path for ½ mile (800 m) to the fine viewpoint (with benches) which overlooks Barafundle Bay, one of Pembrokeshire's prettiest beaches. Go down through the woods to the sands, walk across the beach and ascend a series of steps at its north corner. Beyond the gate and arch at the top of the steps the path crosses a grassy headland on the approach to Stackpole Quay (3). Go through the gate above the quay, turn L at the bottom of the steps and follow the path beside a wall to the car-park.

## 1 Bosherston Lakes

These lakes are part of the Stackpole National Nature Reserve. They wind their way like three long, thin fingers through the undulating greenery close to Broad Haven beach. It comes as a surprise to discover that the lakes are man-made—the valley was dammed in the late eighteenth century—for they blend in harmoniously with their surroundings. The lakes cover 80 acres (32 hectares), the largest expanse of open water in the National Park. They are surrounded by peaceful woodlands, creating a sheltered haven for a wide variety of birds, including swans, mallard, kingfishers and herons. Most of all, though, these lakes are famous for their splendid waterlilies which are at their best in June (the underlying rock is limestone, creating the non-acidic waters ideal for this attractive aquatic plant).

A lakeside path encircles the western lake (a distance of just over 2 miles/3 km), with access to Bosherston, a pretty little village ranged around its Norman cruciform church.

## 2 Stackpole Head

This is one of the most spectacular promontories in Pembrokeshire. Stackpole Head juts out into the sea in a south-easterly direction. At its extremity, it narrows into a small platform of land, with shuddering drops into the waters

*Mowingword headland, on the approach to Stackpole Head*

150

far below. Take care here, especially on a windy day. The limestone cliffs around and about are breeding grounds for razorbills, kittiwakes and guillemots.

3  *Stackpole Quay*

With its solid but small stone jetty, Stackpole Quay is a harbour in miniature, reputedly the smallest in Britain. Limestone was quarried locally—the quay is located almost on the geological dividing line between old red sandstone to the east and carboniferous limestone to the west—and shipped out from the harbour.

The quay is part of a large National Trust holding, based on the old Stackpole Estate, for many centuries the home of the earls of Cawdor. The trust's Stackpole acquisitions include the coastline from the quay to Broad Haven and the Bosherston Lakes. Old farm buildings near the quay have been tastefully renovated by the Trust and now serve as self-catering holiday cottages. The Trust's car-park occupies the site of the former limestone quarry.

*Sheltered, south-facing Broad Haven*

# 1.5

# CARN INGLI IRON AGE HILLFORT

STARTING AND FINISHING
POINT
Small lay-by/car-park on minor
mountain road beside Bedd Morris
standing stone (Pathfinder Sheet SN
03-13/037365)
LENGTH
4 miles (6.5 km)
ASCENT
165 ft (50 m)

The Pembrokeshire Coast National Park is not all seashore. The park's boundary makes one substantial foray inland to enclose the Preseli Hills. The Preselis—*Mynydd Preseli* in Welsh—are an expanse of open hillside and moorland, an eerie upland barrier between the bright sea coasts of North and South Pembrokeshire. A strange atmosphere permeates these empty hills. Legends, mystic tales and speculations surround the Preselis, probably because of the dense concentration of mysterious prehistoric sites to be found here. This easy, attractive walk along the northern flanks of the Preselis will take you across high moorland to a most impressive Iron Age hillfort and a view-point overlooking Newport Bay.

## ROUTE DESCRIPTION (Map 35)

From Bedd Morris *(1)* follow the PFS east across moor. The path soon skirts the edge of a fence (on R), with large, irregularly spaced boundary stones *(2)* marking the route. Continue beside the line of the fence along Mynydd Caregog and within ½ mile (800 m) of the start of the walk turn L, then—within 200 yards (180 m)—turn R, still following the fence.

Within just over ¼ mile (400 m), the route passes the jagged outcrop of Carn Edward on moorland to the R of the fence. Keep walking along the path beside the fence for just over another ¼ mile (400 m). At this point, by a metal-barred gate, the line of the fence veers R down the hillside. From here, continue straight on, following a grassy path across open moorland, climbing gently up to the high ground around the boulder-strewn summit of Carn Ingli *(3)*. On a clear day, the summit will be visible from some distance away, though these hills have their fair share of mist and low cloud.

Skirt the southern slopes of the hillfort. Here, the path disappears as you scramble across difficult ground made up of scattered rocks and bushes directly below the summit. Take care on a wet day, for the rocks can be slippery and thick vegetation masks the rough, underlying terrain.

Approach the summit of the fort from the south-east. Climb up to a fairly level stretch of ground above a group of prehistoric hut circles (the stone circles are clearly visible among the random scattering of rocks and boulders). Head on up to the craggy, pronounced summit of Carn Ingli, from where there are spectacular views north-westwards across Newport Bay, and south-eastwards to the main body of the Preseli Hills.

Retrace your steps back down across the rocks (or skirt the similarly rocky north-western side of the fort) to the open moorland south-west of the fort and rejoin the path back to your starting-point.

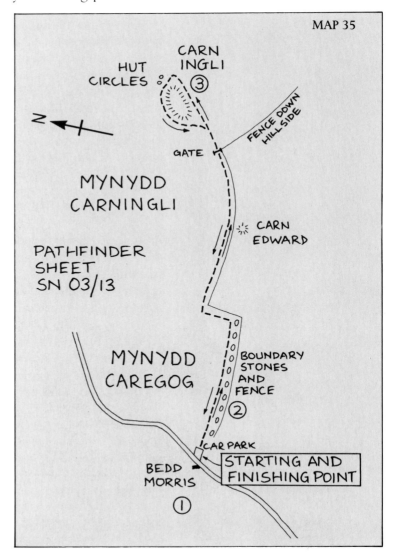

*Opposite: Newport Bay from Carn Ingli*

*1 Bedd Morris*

This roadside pillar is one of the multitude of prehistoric stones scattered across the Preseli Hills. This Bronze Age monolith stands 7½ ft (2.3 m) high. Legend has it that the stone is named after Morris (or Morus), a robber who ambushed people at this spot. He was caught, hanged and lies buried beneath the pillar. Bedd Morris is a boundary marker for two old parishes. On the stone is an inscription which reads 'Llanychlwydog Boundary' (which lies to the south) and 'Newport Boundary' (to the north).

*2 The Beating of the Bounds*

Bedd Morris, and the line of boundary stones along the path, were the focal point for the 'Beating of the Bounds', an event intended to reinforce respect for local borders in medieval times. This traditional ceremony still takes place on the third Friday in August, when a group of locals, on horseback and on foot, meet at Newport Square, proceed to Bedd Morris and then follow the boundary markers across the moor. The 'Beating' is a reference to the old custom of beating the boys in the group to instill in them the location of the boundary marks. The party then returns to Newport to report that the bounds have been followed and that everything has been found to be in order.

*3 Carn Ingli Hillfort*

This impressive Iron Age stronghold is ranged around a 1138-ft (350 m) high point on Carn Ingli Common. The fort, large (9 acres/3.6 hectares) and long (over 400 ft/ 120 m), is a rocky jumble of boulders where man-made ramparts exploit the site's natural defensive strengths by blending into the craggy outcrops, and where features such as terraces, enclosures and stone hut circles can be picked out on the boulder-strewn hillside.

This defended encampment served as a secure stronghold for the Celtic tribesfolk and their cattle in the centuries before and just after the birth of Christ. That much we know, though we can only guess at Carn Ingli's primary function. Was it permanently inhabited or just used as a place of refuge in times of strife? Was it an active centre or simply built to discourage cattle thieves?

*Carn Edward*

# PORTHSTINIAN TO CAERFAI BAY

STARTING POINT
Car-park above St Justinian's Lifeboat
Station (Pathfinder Sheet SM 62-72/
724252)
FINISHING POINT
Car-park above Caerfai Bay
(Pathfinder Sheet 62-72/759244)
LENGTH
6½ miles (10 km)

St David's Peninsula is a magical part of Pembrokeshire. Its storm-tossed, deeply indented coast is dotted with ancient religious sites associated with the early Christian missionaries. The best known among them is, of course, St David, patron saint of Wales. His story is central to our appreciation of this savagely beautiful coastline. David founded a religious community a mile inland at a site on which St David's Cathedral now stands. This purple-stoned cathedral was one of the great historic shrines of Christendom, attracting many pilgrims to this remote south-western corner of Wales, and bestowing the improbable status of a city on a settlement that is no bigger than a village. As with some of the other Pembrokeshire walks, there is a surfeit of stiles on this route. Mention has been made only of those that serve as useful reference points along the way.

## ROUTE DESCRIPTION (Maps 36, 37)

From the car-park, follow the road to a point directly above St Justinian's Lifeboat Station *(1)* and turn L onto the Pembrokeshire Coast Path. The path hugs cliff-tops which, at certain times of the year, are alive with bluebells, foxgloves, thrift and gorse. Within ¼ mile (400 m), pass the little headland and natural arch of Ogof Mary. Cross the stile into the National Trust property of Lower Treginnis.

Follow the path south through a gate and within 200 yards (180 m) the route runs beside an attractive stretch of stone wall infilled with earth and topped with turf. Go through the gate directly above the tiny, rocky Carn-ar-wig Bay (note the rusty winch and old landing stage on the cliffs north of the bay). The path rounds the headland and drops down to a flat, grassy platform of land, the remains of an old copper mine, with superb views across Ramsey Sound and The Bitches to Ramsey Island *(2)*.

Proceed south and south-east along the path across exposed

*Overleaf: The lifeboat station, St Justinian's*

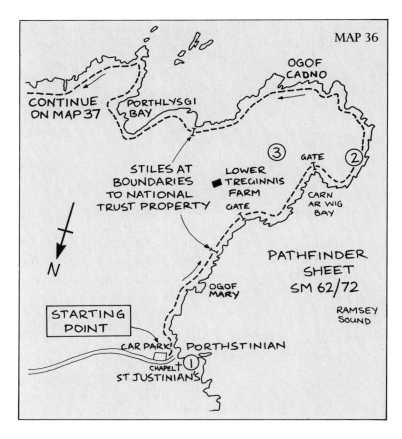

headlands with magnificent views—at Ogof Cadno, for example—across St Bride's Bay and past Newgale Sands toward Marloes and the southern Pembrokeshire coast. Half a mile (800 m) after Ogof Cadno, cross the stile at the eastern boundary of the National Trust's Lower Treginnis property *(3)*.

On the approach to the pebbly Porthlysgi beach, the coast path runs beside green farmlands. Here, the path drops almost to sea level as it rounds Porthlysgi. Continue north-eastwards along more rugged headlands to a precarious-looking natural arch angled into the sea. (Take care, for the path travels close to the cliff-edge at this point.)

Within a few hundred yards, the path passes above bands of razor-sharp rocks on the approach to Porth-clais *(4)*. The inlet of Porth-clais itself is marked by smooth, near-vertical slabs of rock at its mouth. Cross the stile above the breakwater and follow the path down to the quayside. Turn R at the head of the inlet over the bridge and back out along the opposite bank. Turn L at the lime kilns, following the coast-path signpost along the eastern shore of the inlet. At Trwyncynddeiriog ('Furious Point'), ½ mile (800 m) from the harbour, there is another spectacular, exposed headland view-point.

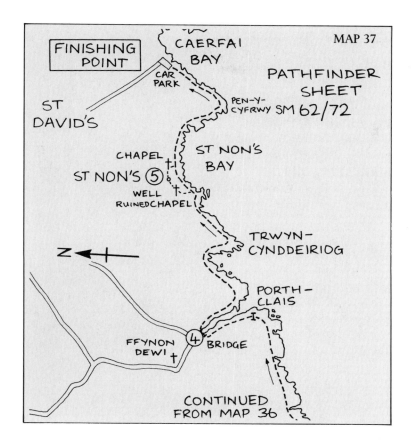

On the approach to St Non's Bay, turn L through a gap in the hedge to take a short deviation off the coast path for St Non's Chapel (ruined), and the Holy Well and Chapel of Our Lady and St Non *(5)*. Go across the field for the ruined chapel, then visit the ancient well which is close to the gate at the top of the field. From here, follow the concrete path a short distance before turning L through a gate for the second chapel. After visiting the chapel, rejoin the concrete path, which after a little way meets up with the coast path.

Follow the path along Pen-y-cyfrwy headland and within ¼ mile (1.2 km) of St Non's you will arrive at the car-park above Caerfai Bay *(6)*.

## 1 St Justinian's

Justinian (Stinian) was a sixth-century hermit, born in Brittany, and reputedly a colleague of St David. Legend has it that this strict disciplinarian retreated to Ramsey Island to devote himself to God. His followers eventually rebelled against his severe rule, cutting off his head, whereupon the saintly Justinian walked across the waters of Ramsey Sound carrying his head in his arms. He was buried at St Justinian's

Chapel (rebuilt in the early sixteenth century) which stands in the private grounds of the coastguard station, but can be seen from the road. His remains were later taken to St David's Cathedral.

The chapel gave the name to Porthstinian (also known locally as St Justinian's), a confined little harbour bounded by jagged rocks and steep cliffs overlooking the dangerous waters of Ramsey Sound. A spectacularly located lifeboat station just manages to squeeze itself in among the rocks. This is the home of the St David's lifeboat, built in 1911–12 for £3000. Porthstinian is also the harbour for day-trips in the tourist season to Ramsey Island.

## 2  Ramsey Island

Ramsey is the Norse name for this lovely, cliff-backed island. Known otherwise as Ynys Dewi—St David's Island—it is about 2 miles (3 km) long and covers some 600 acres (243 hectares). The island, which is a nature reserve, has large sea-bird populations (more than thirty species of bird breed here) and huge numbers—too many—of rabbits. The rocks, coves and inlets around the island are popular with seals, which are particularly conspicuous during September and October, when the Atlantic grey seal hauls itself ashore to breed.

The island is separated from the mainland by the Ramsey Sound (at its narrowest point ½ mile/800 m across), a treacherous stretch of water with a tide-race of up to 8 knots. It is made doubly dangerous by the existence of The Bitches, a ridge of rocks lying close to the surface of the water which claimed the St David's lifeboat *Gem* and three of its crew in October 1910.

## 3  Lower Treginnis

This is one of the many National Trust landholdings in Pembrokeshire. Lower Treginnis incorporates the farmlands and coastline of the little peninsula which juts out south-westwards between St Justinian's and Porthlysgi. This mixed habitat supports a wide variety of wildlife. The cliff-tops are carpeted by colourful maritime grass, pockets of heath cover part of the land, and the rocky coast is a nesting place for yet more sea-birds. The farmer at Lower Treginnis was one of the fifteen survivors when *Gem* went down.

## 4  Porth-clais

This narrow inlet is the perfect sheltered haven for shipping along the stormy western shores of Pembrokeshire. Geologically, it is a valley deepened by glacial melt-water and subsequently drowned by rising sea levels. Historically, it was the harbour for St David's for the many centuries when sea routes served as the main lanes of communication between

Pembrokeshire and the rest of the world. The early Christian missionaries travelling between St David's and Cornwall, Ireland and Brittany must have arrived and departed from here. We know that boats were using Porth-clais in 1385 to off-load cargoes for the cathedral. Between 1585 and 1620 timber was shipped in from Ireland, together with corn, malt and wool from, respectively, mid-Wales, Bristol and Barnstaple. There were also exports: wheat, barley, corn and rye to the West Country. Well into the twentieth century, coal was brought into Porth-clais, then transported by cart to St David's, a mile (1.6 km) away. The kilns along the harbour were used to produce lime (by burning limestone and coal) which was spread on the farmlands to sweeten the acid soil.

A little way along the road leading north-westwards from Porth-clais is Ffynnon Dewi (David's Well), where St David was baptized by Elvis, Bishop of Munster.

### 5  St Non

St Non, or Nonnita, was the mother of St David. Legend has it that David was born on the grassy slopes above St Non's Bay during a great storm around AD 500. The spot is marked by the ruins of a chapel of obscure origin, traditionally associated with St Non, which may date from before the Norman Conquest. The chapel was probably abandoned in the middle of the sixteenth century.

A small, white statue of St Non stands nearby, close to the holy well dedicated to her. This famous well, the waters of which were said to have miraculous powers for healing eye diseases, was much visited by pilgrims to St David's.

The Chapel of Our Lady and St Non, although built in the style of Pembrokeshire chapels of 500 years ago, dates from the 1930s. This little chapel with its sturdy, buttressed walls is associated with the larger building standing on the hillside above. This is St Non's Retreat, a centre for spiritual renewal, which was completed in 1929.

### 6  Caerfai Bay

This beautiful, sheltered bay of firm sands is the closest beach to St David's. Stones from the quarries in the cliffs (below the site now occupied by the car-park) were used to build St David's Cathedral.

Limekilns at Porth-clais

# 2.7

# Dale Peninsula

STARTING AND FINISHING
POINT
Car park beside Dale beach
(Pathfinder Sheet SM 80-90/812058)
LENGTH
7 miles (11.3 km)

The satellite view of Pembrokeshire reveals a giant peninsula. If the camera were to come in closer, it would scan a coastline made up of many smaller peninsulas. Among Pembrokeshire's proliferation of promontories, the Dale Peninsula stands out as something special. Located at the mouth of Milford Haven in the far-flung south-western corner of the park, well away from mainstream tourist traffic, Dale is peaceful and unexplored. Its footpaths do not have the well-trodden look to them that you find in other parts of the park. And Dale's neat, self-contained shape offers the opportunity—rare in Pembrokeshire—of following a circular route.

This walk takes in a variety of splendid coastal scenery—everything from windy, west-facing cliffs to sheltered bays in the calm Haven—and there is the promise of an exceptionally attractive sandy beach on the return leg to placate the younger members of the family. There are many stiles on this walk—far too many to mention individually. The ones specifically mentioned in the text are useful reference points along the route.

## Route Description (Maps 38–40)

From the beach, walk west along the one-way system, past the Dale Sailing Company and Post House Hotel. Turn R at the T-junction at the end of the housing estate and within 150 yards (140 m) turn L at the PFS along an unmade road. Within a further 150 yards (140 m) cross a stile, following the PFS, and walk through a field for ¼ mile (400 m) to the stile above Westdale Bay, a west-facing beach popular with surfers.

After the stile turn L along the coast path and climb a series of steps up to Great Castle Head, which has impressive remains of an Iron Age fort (1). This first stretch of the path is well defined though thickly vegetated with tall grasses, gorse, fern, foxgloves, thrift and nettles. Looking east across the narrow neck of the peninsula, you see the somewhat incongruous panorama of Dale's natural beauty set against a background of

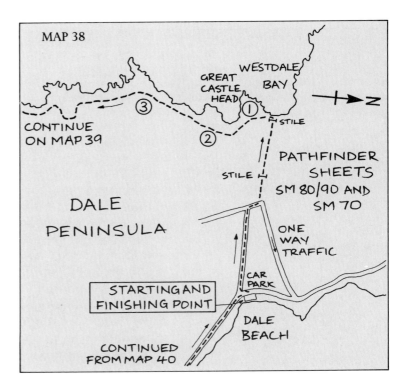

the oil and petrochemical installations (2) that line the banks of the Milford Haven waterway.

The path then runs along the top of the cliff which skirts a rocky, exposed coastline and there are fine views westwards to Skokholm Island and north-westwards along Marloes Sands, past Gateholm Island, to Skomer Island (3). A profusion of wild flowers, including yellow rockrose, thrift, deadly nightshade, campion and bird's-foot trefoil, brings splashes of colour to the cliff-top grasslands at various times of the year.

Go straight on at the signpost for Kete car-park. The path then runs along the top of the craggy, inaccessible Frenchman's Bay. The cliffs are loose, steep and close to the path at this point, so do not stray off the designated route. At the stile just beyond the rock-bound indentation with the unappealing but unforgettable name of The Vomit, turn R along a metalled road for St Ann's Head at the mouth of Milford Haven (4).

Go past the coastguard station and marine rescue centre (5). Turn L at the gate across the road on the approach to the lighthouse and follow the line of the fence (there is no public access to the lighthouse) which runs alongside the road and then beside a row of houses. At the end of the row, turn L and follow the path across a field. Within 250 yards (225 m), the path runs alongside the wall of some old allotments. Bear half L at the end of the wall signposted 'coast path' and shortly cross a stile.

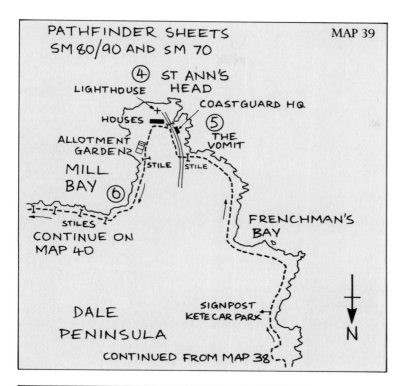

PATHFINDER SHEETS
SM 80/90 AND SM 70

MAP 39

④ ST ANN'S HEAD

LIGHTHOUSE

COASTGUARD HQ

HOUSES

⑤ THE VOMIT

ALLOTMENT GARDENS

STILE    STILE

MILL BAY

⑥

STILES

CONTINUE ON MAP 40

FRENCHMAN'S BAY

DALE PENINSULA

SIGNPOST KETE CAR PARK

N

CONTINUED FROM MAP 38

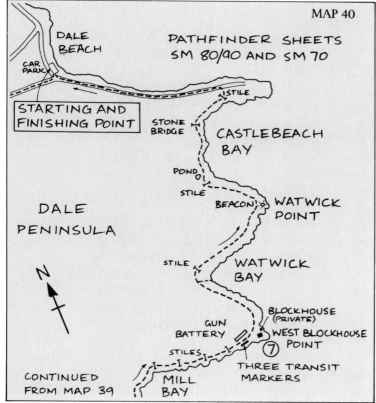

MAP 40

DALE BEACH

CAR PARK

PATHFINDER SHEETS
SM 80/90 AND SM 70

STARTING AND FINISHING POINT

STILE

STONE BRIDGE

CASTLEBEACH BAY

POND

STILE

BEACON

WATWICK POINT

DALE PENINSULA

N

STILE

WATWICK BAY

BLOCKHOUSE (PRIVATE)

GUN BATTERY

WEST BLOCKHOUSE POINT

⑦

STILES

THREE TRANSIT MARKERS

CONTINUED FROM MAP 39

MILL BAY

Overleaf: *Westdale Bay, a popular surfing beach*

Continue along the path, dropping down into a dingle from which there is access to Mill Bay *(6)*. Climb back up onto the grassy hill above the bay. For the next ¼ mile (400 m) or so, the well-defined path crosses a number of stiles as it runs along field boundaries near the cliff edge. Cross yet another stile—straight on, signposted 'coast path'—at the western approach to West Blockhouse Point and continue past three tall transit markers for shipping.

Here, the path runs between an abandoned gun battery (on the higher ground) and the Victorian West Blockhouse below (private) *(7)*. Continue for just over ⅓ mile (500 m). At this point you can take a detour R down to the superb, sheltered, golden-sanded beach at Watwick Bay, which is idyllic on a warm summer's day. Rejoin the path and at the stile above the bay turn R along a wide path beside fields to Watwick Point, with its lofty beacon tower.

The path then skirts a field above the pretty, wooded coast which fringes Castlebeach Bay. After you cross a stile, the path drops down almost immediately to an irrigation pond on the L. Within 20 yards (18 m) of the pond, bear half R. Follow the path around the southern stretch of the bay—wooded and bushy in parts, but always well defined—descending to a small shingle-and-sand beach. Cross the stone bridge at the bottom of the steps beside the beach and go back up another series of steps, then follow the path across open headland. Within 100 yards (90 m) of the metalled road, turn L over the stile, then turn L again along the road back to Dale, just over ¾ mile (1.2 km) away.

*1 Iron Age fort*

Ancient promontory forts are not uncommon along the Pembrokeshire coast. This fine example, dating from about 100 BC, has huge banks and ditches. Its defences also incorporate, quite ingeniously, sudden changes in the level of the land caused by geological faulting.

*2 Oil and petrochemicals*

Pembrokeshire's coastal harmonies are interrupted by a massively discordant intrusion along the banks of the Milford Haven waterway. Silver stacks pierce the skies above modern jetties and a tangle of feeder pipes which service alien-looking installations where oil is stored and processed. Milford Haven's deep-water channel and the advent of bigger and bigger tankers attracted the major oil companies to its banks. Since the first refinery was opened in 1960, the Haven has grown to become Britain's major oil port, handling some 35 million tons of crude oil and its associated products annually.

Giant supertankers glide in and out of the Haven—the headlands along east Dale are ideal vantage-points for ship-spotters—the only natural harbour in southern Britain able to accommodate them. Unwelcome though the presence of this industry is in strict environmental terms, we must give due regard to its role in boosting our modern economy. It should also be said that the Haven enjoys a much-admired anti-oil-pollution record.

3 *Skokholm and Skomer Islands*

Pembrokeshire's sea-bird life is particularly prolific on these two islands. Their strange-sounding names are of Norse origin (as is that of Dale itself, which means 'valley'). Skokholm, the smaller and more remote, was the site of Britain's first bird observatory, established in 1933. Both islands are nature reserves of international repute. Skomer, for example, has one of north-west Europe's finest populations of sea-birds, its occupants including shags, razorbills, fulmars, puffins, oystercatchers, kittiwakes, guillemots and an exceptionally large colony of Manx shearwaters. Skomer is the easier island to get to: there are regular boat trips in summer from Martin's Haven near Marloes.

4 *The Milford Haven waterway*

The deep-water Milford Haven has been recognized for centuries as one of the world's finest harbours. Admiral Lord Nelson was one of many to sing its praises as a safe, sheltered anchorage. The Haven is a classic *ria*, or drowned river valley. When Britain's glaciers disappeared, the water level in the Haven increased substantially, turning it into a deep-water inlet. Even at low tide, its waters are over 50 ft (15 m) deep.

5 *St Ann's Head Coastguard Station and Marine Rescue Centre*

This headland guards the mouth of Milford Haven, protecting its waters from the fierce westerly gales that often blow. Wind speeds of over 100 mph (160 km/h) have been recorded here at least five times since 1946, and there are usually over thirty severe gales a year. Also playing a protective role is an extensive coastguard complex, which includes a powerful lighthouse, offices and housing for personnel. This coastguard station, with its sophisticated equipment, is the modern equivalent of the flaming beacon which burned in ages past at St Ann's Head, warning ships of the dangerous reefs at the approach to the Haven.

6 *Mill Bay*

This obscure, rocky little bay witnessed a dramatic episode in the founding of the mighty Tudor dynasty. It was the landing-point, on 7 August 1485, of Harri Tudur, who was shortly to become Henry VII, first of the Tudor monarchs. Harri, a Welshman born at Pembroke Castle, returned from exile in France with an army of 2000 men. After landing in Mill Bay, he marched through Wales to England's Midlands, gathering more support along the way. At Bosworth Field, on 22 August, he achieved a famous victory over Richard III to take the throne of England.

7 *Fortifications along the Haven*

The West Blockhouse is one of the many fortifications and gun emplacements along the waterway. The Haven has been a busy sea route since ancient times. Serious attempts to defend its waters had to wait until the mid-nineteenth century, spurred on by the potential threat which France posed to the naval dockyard at Pembroke Dock. West Blockhouse was one of the series of nine forts and batteries built at this time. Completed in 1857, it had a garrison of 80 men and formed part of the defences of the outer Haven. The fort also saw use during both world wars, but was abandoned in 1950. The gun emplacements can still be visited, though the fort, on West Blockhouse Point below the path, is not accessible to the public.

*Frenchman's Bay along Dale's exposed west coast*

# Appendices

## Access for the Walker

It is important to remember that the designation National Park does not alter the ownership of private land within such a park's boundaries. The laws of access and trespass apply just as much within the park as outside it.

One of the main objectives of the 1949 National Parks and Access to the Countryside Act was to secure the right to roam at will over uncultivated mountain and moorland. In the event, however, neither the Act nor the designation National Park confers this right.

The walker in both the Brecon Beacons and along the Pembrokeshire coast is lucky in that access is not a major problem, though the other parks have their different local characteristics. A large part of the open hillsides and mountains in the Beacons is common land and the walker enjoys access to much of this either by public right-of-way or by the tradition of *de facto* access (see page 18).

In Pembrokeshire, walkers benefit from the long-distance right-of-way that exists along the coastal footpath.

All the walks in this book use either public rights-of-way, areas of *de facto* access or acceptable alternative routes.

Finally, it should be borne in mind that, because of heavy use, paths in the more popular parts of the Brecon Beacons and Pembrokeshire become badly eroded, making footpath maintenance necessary from time to time. If you encounter diversion signs, please follow them rather than sticking rigidly to the routes given in the text.

## Maps

There is a wide range of maps covering both the Brecon Beacons and the Pembrokeshire coast. For walking purposes, by far the best are produced by the Ordnance Survey.

The Brecon Beacons National Park is fortunate in being the subject of the excellent Outdoor Leisure series on the scale 1:25 000 (4 cm to 1 km or approximately 2½ in to 1 mile). The western, central and eastern Beacons are covered by sheets 12, 11 and 13 respectively. Most of the park is also contained on sheet 160 of the Landranger 1:50 000 series (2 cm to 1 km or approximately 1¼ in to 1 mile).

The more localized Pathfinder series, again on the scale 1:25 000, covers the Pembrokeshire coast. The sheets relevant to the walks in this book are Cardigan and Dinas Head (SN 04/14), Newport and Eglwyswrw (SN 03/13), Fishguard (SM 83/93), St David's and Ramsey Island (SM 62/72), Skomer Island (SM 70), Milford Haven (SM 80/90) and Castlemartin and St Govan's Head (SR 89/99). The coast is also covered by sheet numbers 145, 157 and 158 of the Landranger 1:50 000 series.

All map references in this book have been based on the Ordnance Survey grid system.

# *Safety*

The routes described in this guide vary considerably in both length and difficulty. Some of the easy walks should, with reasonable care, be safe at any time of the year and in almost any weather conditions; the more difficult walks on the other hand, using the high moorland cross-country routes, can be arduous in bad weather. These should be undertaken in winter only by groups of well-equipped and experienced walkers.

It cannot be emphasized too strongly that weather conditions can change very rapidly. What is a drizzle in a valley could be a blizzard on the moor top. Select clothing and equipment for the worst weather you may encounter. Two competent rescue teams are available by police call-out. If you meet with an accident, either to one of your own party or by discovering someone else injured, give what First Aid you are capable of administering. If necessary, shelter the casualty. Write down the grid reference of the incident, and then locate the nearest village or telephone. Ideally two people should go for assistance, leaving someone behind with the casualty, but obviously the decision will be determined by the number in the party.

The golden rules which will ensure walkers' safety in mountain and moorland areas (and, to a lesser extent, the easier coastal routes) are:

## DO
Carry appropriate clothing and equipment, which should be in sound condition.
Carry map and compass and be practised in their use.
Leave a note of your intended route with a responsible person (and keep to it!).
Report your return as soon as possible.
Keep warm, but not overwarm, at all times.
Eat nourishing foods and rest at regular intervals.
Avoid becoming exhausted.
Know First Aid and the correct procedures in case of accident or illness.
Obtain a weather forecast before you start.

## DO NOT
Go out on your own unless you are very experienced. Three is a good number.
Leave any member of the party behind on a mountain or moor unless help has to be summoned.
Explore old mine workings or caves or climb cliffs (except scrambling ridges).
Attempt routes which are beyond your skill and experience.

# Giving a Grid Reference

Giving a grid reference is an excellent way of 'pinpointing' a feature, such as a church or mountain summit, on an Ordnance Survey map.

Grid lines, which are used for this purpose, are shown on the 1:25 000 Outdoor Leisure, 1:25 000 Pathfinder and 1:50 000 Landranger maps produced by the Ordnance Survey; these are the maps most commonly used by walkers. Grid lines are the thin blue lines one kilometre apart going vertically and horizontally across the map producing a network of small squares. Each line, whether vertical or horizontal, is given a number from 00 to 99, with the sequence repeating itself every 100 lines. The 00 lines are slightly thicker than the others thus producing large squares each side representing 100 km and made up of 100 small squares. Each of these large squares is identified by two letters. The entire network of lines covering the British Isles, excluding Ireland, is called the National Grid.

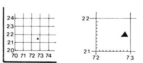

FIGURE 4  Giving a
grid reference

The left-hand diagram above shows a corner of an Ordnance Survey 1:50 000 Landranger map which contains a Youth Hostel. Using this map,

the method of determining a grid reference is as follows:

*Step 1*
Holding the map in the normal upright position, note the number of the 'vertical' grid line to the left of the hostel. This is 72.

*Step 2*
Now imagine that the space between this grid line and the adjacent one to the right of the hostel is divided into ten equal divisions (the right-hand part of the diagram shows this). Estimate the number of these 'tenths' that the hostel lies to the right of the left-hand grid line. This is 8. Add this to the number found in Step 1 to make 728.

*Step 3*
Note the number of the grid line below the hostel and add it on to the number obtained above. This is 21, so that the number becomes 72821.

*Step 4*
Repeat Step 2 for the space containing the hostel, but now in a vertical direction. The final number to be added is 5, making 728215. This is called a six-figure grid reference. This, coupled with the number or name of the appropriate Landranger or Outdoor Leisure map, will enable the Youth Hostel to be found.

A full grid reference will also include the identification of the appropriate 100 kilometre square of the National Grid; for example, SD 728215. This information is given in the margin of each map.

# Countryside Access Charter

YOUR RIGHTS OF WAY ARE

Public footpaths—on foot only. Sometimes way-marked in yellow

Bridleways—on foot, horseback and pedal cycle. Sometimes waymarked in blue

Byways (usually old roads), most 'Roads Used as Public Paths' and, of course, public roads—all traffic

Use maps, signs and waymarks. Ordnance Survey Pathfinder and Landranger maps show most public rights-of-way.

ON RIGHTS-OF-WAY YOU CAN

Take a pram, pushchair or wheelchair if practicable

Take a dog (on a lead or under close control)

Take a short route round an illegal obstruction or remove it sufficiently to get past

YOU HAVE A RIGHT TO GO FOR RECREATION TO

Public parks and open spaces—on foot

Most commons near older towns and cities—on foot and sometimes on horseback

Private land where the owner has a formal agreement with the local authority

IN ADDITION YOU CAN USE BY LOCAL OR ESTABLISHED CUSTOM OR CONSENT (BUT ASK FOR ADVICE IF YOU'RE UNSURE)

Many areas of open country like moorland, fell and coastal areas, especially those of the National Trust and some commons

Some woods and forests, especially those owned by the Forestry Commission

Country Parks and picnic sites

Most beaches

Canal towpaths

Some private paths and tracks. Consent sometimes extends to riding horses and pedal cycles

FOR YOUR INFORMATION

County councils and London boroughs maintain and record rights-of-way, and register commons

Obstruction, dangerous animals, harassment and misleading signs on rights-of-way are illegal and you should report them to the county council

Paths across fields can be ploughed, but must normally be reinstated within two weeks

Landowners can require you to leave land to which you have no right of access

Motor vehicles are normally permitted only on roads, byways and some 'Roads Used as Public Paths'

Follow any local byelaws

AND, WHEREVER YOU GO, FOLLOW THE COUNTRY CODE

Enjoy the countryside and respect its life and work

Guard against all risk of fire

Fasten all gates

Keep your dogs under close control

Keep to public paths across farmland

Use gates and stiles to cross fences, hedges and walls

Leave livestock, crops and machinery alone

Take your litter home

Help to keep all water clean

Protect wildlife, plants and trees

Take special care on country roads

Make no unnecessary noise

This Charter is for practical guidance in England and Wales only. It was prepared by the Countryside Commission.

# Addresses of Useful Organizations

## 1 NATIONAL PARKS

Brecon Beacons National Park
7 Glamorgan Street
Brecon
Powys LD3 7DP
Brecon (0874) 4437

Brecon Beacons Mountain Centre
Nr Libanus
Brecon
Powys LD3 8ER
Brecon (0874) 3366

In addition to the Mountain Centre, open all year, there are Information Centres open seasonally at Abergavenny (0873–3254), Brecon (0874–4437) and Llandovery (0550–20693). The National Park is also responsible for the Craig-y-nos Country Park, open all year, near Abercraf (0639–730395) where an Information Point is manned in the summer months.

The Brecon Beacons National Park also runs the Danywenallt Study Centre, a residential field study centre at Aber, near Talybont-on-Usk (087487–677).

Pembrokeshire Coast National Park
County Offices
Haverfordwest
Dyfed SA61 1QZ
Haverfordwest (0437) 764591

A network of Information Centres, open seasonally, is spread throughout the National Park. The locations are: Newport (0239–820912), St David's (0437–720392), Broad Haven (0437–781412), Pembroke (0646–682148), Haverfordwest (0437–66141), Tenby (0834–2402), Kilgetty (0834–811411). In addition to these National Park centres, there is a Tourist Information Centre at Fishguard (0348–873484) and a National Park Information Agency at the Dale Sailing Company shop in Dale village.

## 2 NATIONAL TRUST

The National Trust (South Wales)
The King's Head
Llandeilo
Dyfed SA19 6BN
Llandeilo (0558) 822800

The National Trust
36 Queen Anne's Gate
London SW1H 9AS
01–222 9251

## 3 OTHER USEFUL ADDRESSES

*The Brecon Beacons*

Brecknock Naturalists' Trust
c/o Chapel House
Llechfaen
Brecon
Powys LD3 7SP
Llanfrynach (087486) 688

*The Pembrokeshire coast*

Dyfed Archaeological Trust
Old Carmarthen Art College
Church Lane
Carmarthen
Dyfed
Carmarthen (0267) 231667

Dyfed Wildlife Trust
7 Market Street
Haverfordwest
Dyfed SA61 1NF
Haverfordwest (0437) 5462

Field Studies Council
Orielton Field Centre
Nr Pembroke
Dyfed
Castlemartin (064681) 225

*also:* Dale Fort Field Centre
Dale
Dyfed
(06465) 205

*General*

Council for National Parks
45 Shelton Street
London WC2 9HJ
01–240 3603

Countryside Commission
John Dower House
Crescent Place
Cheltenham
Gloucestershire GL50 3RA
Cheltenham (0242) 521381

Countryside Commission Office for Wales
Ladywell House
Newtown
Powys SY16 1RD
Newtown (0686) 26799

Long Distance Walkers Association
7 Ford Drive
Yarnfield
Stone
Staffordshire ST15 ORP
Stone (0785) 760684

Nature Conservancy Council
Dyfed-Powys Regional Office
Plas Gogerddan
Aberystwyth
Dyfed SY23 3EB
Aberystwyth (0970) 828551

Nature Conservancy Council
South Wales Regional Office
43 The Parade
Roath
Cardiff
South Glamorgan CF2 3AB
Cardiff (0222) 485111

Ramblers' Association
1/5 Wandsworth Road
London SW8 2XX
01–582 6878

Wales Tourist Board
PO Box 1
Cardiff
South Glamorgan CF1 2XN
Cardiff (0222) 227281

Youth Hostels Association (England and Wales)
Trevelyan House
8 St Stephen's Hill
St Albans
Hertfordshire AL1 2DY
St Albans (0727) 55215

Youth Hostels Association (Regional Office)
Regional Office
1 Cathedral Road
Cardiff CF1 9HA
Cardiff (0222) 231370

The Camping and Caravanning Club of Great Britain and
Ireland Ltd.
11 Lower Grosvenor Place
London SW1W 0EY
01–828 1012

# INDEX

Place names only are included. Page numbers in *italics* refer to illustrations.